Woods, Places, Bears 'n Faces

PETER D. CLARK

c. Peter D. Clark, 1995

All rights reserved. No part of this work may be reproduced or used in any form by any means, electronic or mechanical, including photocopying, recording, or any information storage and retrieval system, without the prior written permission of the author.

Published by Penniac Books, RR#9, Site 2, Comp.11, Fredericton, N.B. E3B 4X9.

I.S.B.N. 0-9699648-0-3

Front Cover Photo by Sylvie Malo-Clark.
Back Cover Photo by Prof. Gary Brown.
The "Bear-Man" photo donated by Eldon M. Robichaud
Printed in Canada by Centennial Print & Litho Ltd.

Canadian Cataloguing in Publication Data

Clark, Peter D. (Peter Dale), 1950-

   Woods, Places, Bears 'n Faces

   Includes index.
   ISBN 0-9699648-0-3

1. New Brunswick — Anecdotes. I. Title.

FC2461.8.C52 1995   971.5 1   C95-950151-7
F1042.6.C52 1995

1. Stories.
2. New Brunswick Folklore.
I. Title. "Woods, Places, Bears 'n Faces"

Acknowledgements:

Several people have been instrumental in the writing of this book. Dr. Dalton London and Vella Mooers Schwartz played a major role in helping to organize and edit the manuscript while June Campbell was busy doing the typing. I'd like to mention my deep appreciation to each and every artist for their wonderful contributions. Special thanks to the helpful staff at both the Provincial and Legislative Archives as well as *The Daily Gleaner* and *The Grand Lake Mirror*. Many special thanks to the late Charlie Clayton Sr. and Ernie Hall as well as Johnny Washburn, Eva Searle, Levi Grant, George McDonald, Murray Sargeant, and Jack Fenety. I'd personally like to thank the many individuals whom I interviewed for their valuable information. In closing I'd like to say that Pat Delong lent his ear and advice from the beginning to the end and his continuous reassurance was a guiding light.

– Peter D. Clark

This book is dedicated to my father, the late Harold Clark, and my brother Ron with whom I've shared many magical moments in the woods and on the waters of New Brunswick.

CONTENTS:

Malabeam	1
The Yarnin' Barber Johnny Washburn	5
Maggie Jean Chestnut	21
The Riverview Arms	26
"The Bear Man"	31
Henry Braithwaite	33
My Biggest Trout	36
Do Bright Salmon Ever Eat?	38
Dry Fly Fishing	41
Levi Grant	43
The Bear Story	48
Rippling Rivers	53
Trout Fishing Years Ago	55
My First Teaching Position	60
Reddy Fox 1913-1973	63
Sam Satter	68
Fact & Fancy	72
Charlie Clayton's Camps	74
The Nondescript Davey, called the Man Bear	80

ILLUSTRATORS:

Carol-Ann Smith	3
Nick Gallagher	6, 39
Bruno Bobak	9, 11, 13
Phil Vincent	22
Ian Smith	25
Ray Bailey	34
Michiel Oudemans	37
Jamie McFarlane	58
Alex McGibbon	45, 62, 65, 69
Corrine Hersey	50
Jeff Starr	75

Malabeam

The Maliseet Indians have lived here in New Brunswick for thousands of years. Until quite recently, their only written language was confined to rock formations, stoneblades, spearheads and pictographs. The natives believed in a supreme being which was in all things – the trees, grasses, mountains and all the four legged animals that walked the earth. They felt that one should know, love and fear the great spirit and live as the spirit intended. The Indians believed that the trees talk – if you know how to listen, you can hear them predict the weather, know about the animals and sometimes delve into the mysteries of the great spirit.

The Indian people believed that all living things served a purpose in life. The eagle and its feathers were revered as a symbol of power. And to travel quickly in their unspoiled wilderness, the Indians built the most beautiful and functional watercraft ever created – the canoe. The canoe figures prominently in one of the most remarkable stories to come down to us from another age.

A plaque at the Grand Falls Tourism office gives the reader a fleeting, intriguing glimpse into the legend which has been passed down from generation to generation.

"A Maliseet maiden saved her people from destruction by luring an attacking party of Mohawks over the Grand Falls"

The Maliseet nation were a peaceful tribe that inhabited an area just above and below Grand Falls. They spent their time hunting, fishing, harvesting, and in organizing cultural events. Housed in wigwams, they lived a simple, harmonious life. Up until the time of our story the Maliseets were at peace with all of the other tribes in the region, including those living in the lower St. Lawrence River Basin.

One day the elder Sakotis and his daughter, Malabeam, ventured up the St. John River for an outing. They were camping on an island when suddenly the air was pierced by the screams and war whoops of the blood–thirsty Mohawks. A sharp flint–tipped arrow struck old Sakotis in the heart. Poor Malabeam watched in horror as her father gasped his last breath. She ran into the woods but was quickly captured and given an ultimatum. She was told that she must lead the Mohawk tribe to her village or face torture and possibly death. By cooperating, her life would be spared, providing she wed a Mohawk. She knew that her fate was sealed for she could never betray her native brothers and sisters. She ostensibly agreed to help and devised the only plan possible. Darkness was fast approaching and she instructed the 300 warriors to fasten their canoes in four lines with her in the centre, leading the way.

The Mohawks were bedecked with their war colours. Indeed, many of the Mohawk braves wore three eagle feathers as a sign of being brave hunters and warriors. Thoughts of vengeance and destruction were on their minds. Their chants and martial songs echoed from the shores in the still of the night.

Slowly their birch–bark canoes slithered through the ominous black waters. Before long there was a slight roll like thunder in the distance. The noise increased as they neared the falls. Some of the men were sleeping, others became slightly alarmed. Malabeam told them the noise was coming from a stream entering the river.

Gradually the noises awakened the sleeping and set panic and terror in the hearts of even the bravest. The chief and this army were caught in the heavy current with the noise turning into a deafening roar.

There was a scream from Malabeam – "Prepare to meet your deaths – you Mohawks".

There was a wild plunge – a sudden shock – shrieks of death became one with the deafening rumble of the mighty cataract. Canoes broke into pieces – as bodies landed on the rocks and boiling foam. Not a soul survived the carnage.

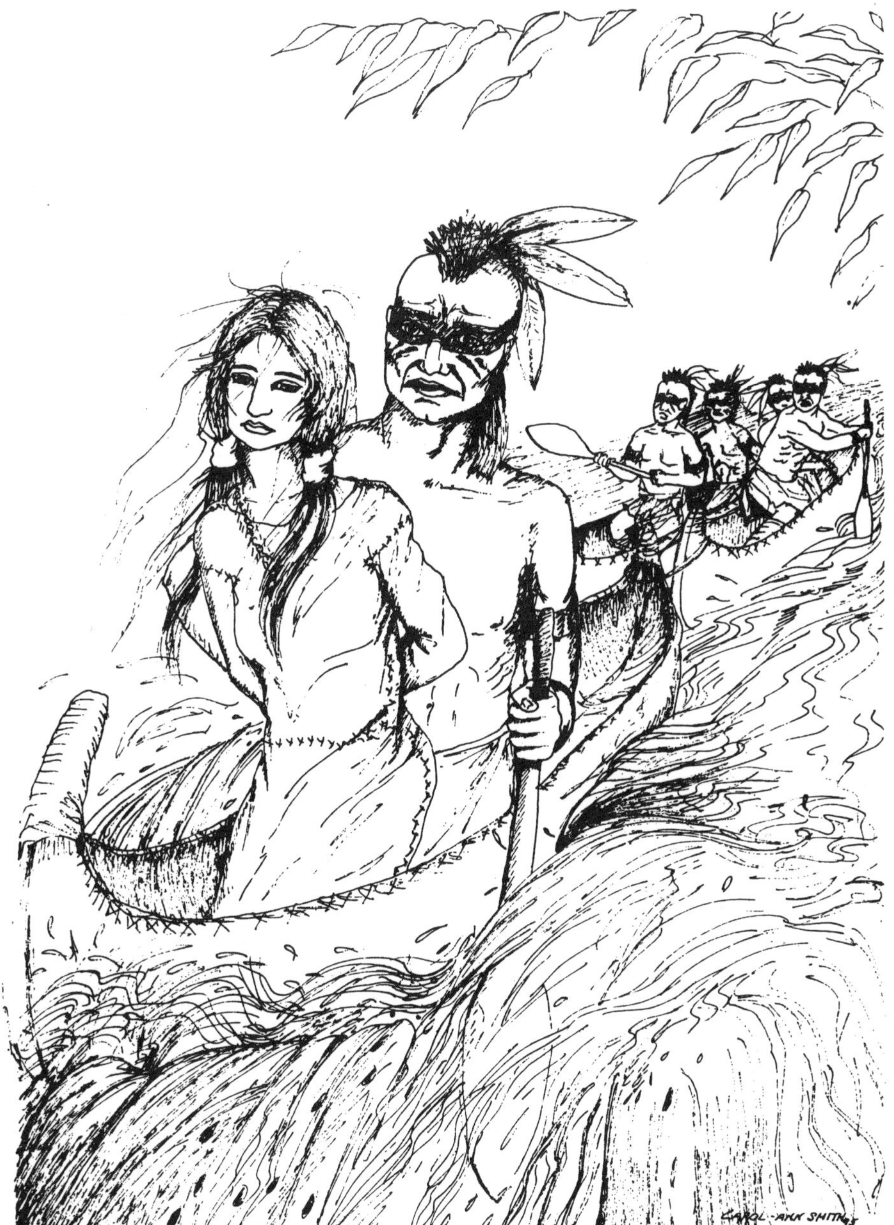
CAROL-ANN SMITH

Malabeam had saved a nation but was unable to save herself. The Maliseets never recovered her body. She lies in the dark river's embrace. The bravest Indian maiden's story is told and sung by many to this very day.

The Yarnin' Barber Johnny Washburn

John has told jokes and stories on national television, national CBC radio and was interviewed by the press before his retirement.

Indeed, John Washburn's name is synonymous with yarnin'. He hails from Howard, near Blackville where he declares "the bus is bigger than the post office". He claims to have been born December 3, 1925 under a sink, declares that he still remembers hearing the water runnin'. He comes from a large family of 6 girls and 4 boys and was raised in a farmhouse about a mile from the Cains River in front of Washburn's Island. He remembers tellin' tales at a tender age because everyone else was. As a young man he worked as a guide. He went as far as grade 10 in school. He graduated from St. Andrews Trade School in 1969. He jokes about his first real job working in a pantyhose factory, pullin' down 20,000 a year.

John actually worked as a lineman for N.B.Tel, Canadian National Telegraph and Delta Electric. One day while sliding down a frozen telephone pole in Arctic temperatures he made a decision to take up barbering. He was employed by Bert Holyoke in Nashwaaksis, then with Ed MacLean (1966–70) and then at 68 Regent Street where Tom and Ed McCarty had set up a barber shop. In 1971 he bought out the McCarty brothers and began working on his own.

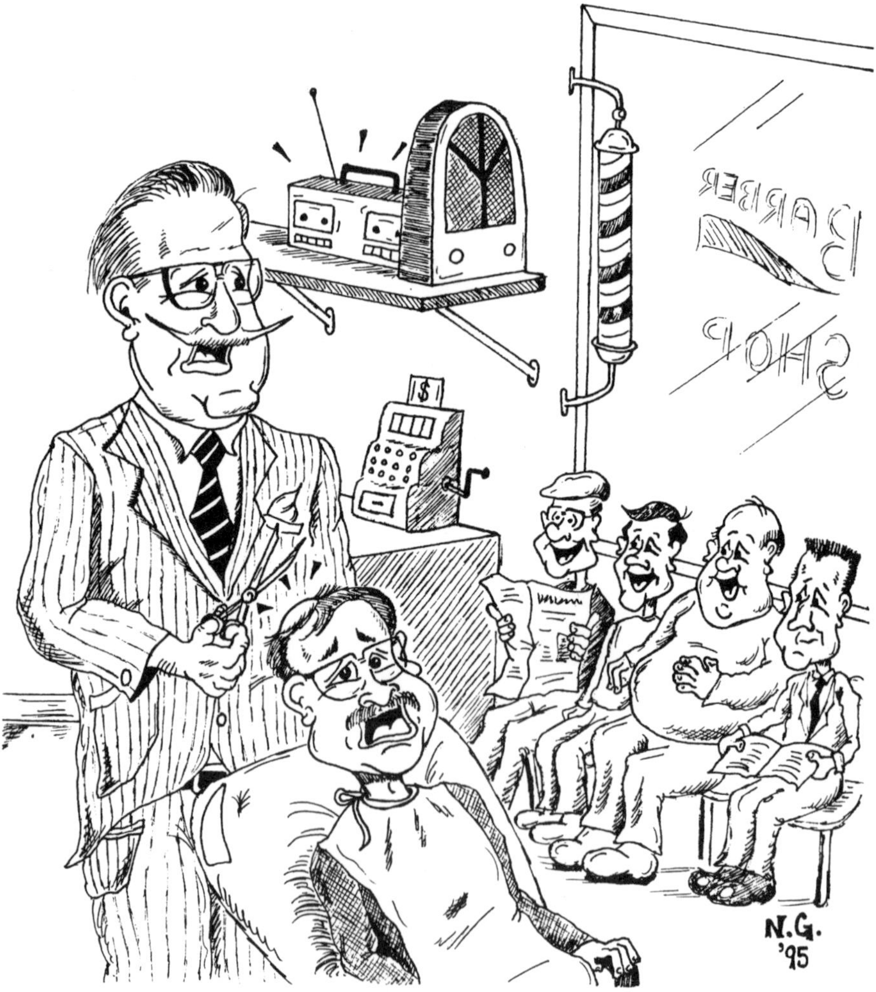
BARBER
SHOP
$
N.G.
'95

John is tall in stature, silver–haired, immaculate in apparel and sports a long waxed handlebar mustache. John's spit shined shoes were, and are to this day, a trademark. On any given day his shoes were such that if you looked down you could see your reflection. He was an expert in his field having clipped hair for 25 years. John loved his job and in particular enjoyed meeting people. Some of his clients affectionately nicknamed him the "Demon Barber of Regent Street". One fact is certain – his business flourished with characters such as Pat Delong, Art Lank (the Quacker), Cameron Munn, Don Daley, and Rupert Morehouse to name a few regulars. Topics such as politics, religion and sex were openly discussed and debated. It was a "no–holds–barred" barber shop that could make a minister blush. At times it was down–right dangerous to receive a hair–cut, as you will discover later.

John's barbershop was a place of good–natured camaraderie. Some individuals stopped by for a visit to find out the latest gossip or joke which John could deliver with flair. He continually lamented about the enormous costs of feeding the pigeons and sparrows which frequented his doorsteps. He also has been known to give haircuts on credit knowing full well that the expected fee has gone up in smoke with the exit of certain clients. John also cut hair for the Training School, Reformatory and the York County Jail. He had a plaque on his wall from the J Division of the R.C.M.P. thanking him for "25 years of clippin' and yarnin'." John retired January 1, 1991, much to the chagrin of his many friends and customers.

Today John enjoys the retirement life in Silverwood just on the outer fringes of Fredericton, N.B. He enjoys his favourite hobbies of fishin', huntin' and yarnin'.. though John claims to this day that he has never told a yarn in his life. John is often seen at the Boyce Farmers' Market Saturday mornings.

In the following pages I have attempted to write about some situations and events as told by Johnny which are the honest gospel and some others which are close to being credible.

Fishin' the Miramichi with Johnny Washburn

I remember fishin' salmon at my pool near Blackville when a man could keep a salmon – oh about 1976. There was an American sport fishin' out of a boat with one of the local guides. They had no business being on my pool but I kept my trap shut.

I was wading near shore when I hooked a nice salmon – I'd say around 15 pounds. The American was tickled pink. He took to whoopin' and hollerin' – you'd swear he was the one who hooked the fish.

He yelled, "Do you mind if I come ashore to watch you play that big salmon?"

"Suit yourself", I snapped, "It ain't no big deal."

Well – we talked about one thing and another as I battled this magnificent beauty. He let me know that he was from New York and had caught many a trout. This was his first trip to New Brunswick fishin' salmon. He said that he had tied up over 200 assorted flies for the trip. He had Conrads, Butterflies, Rusty Rats, Cossebooms, Royal Wulfs, White Wulfs, Bombers, etc. He asked me if I tied my own. I noticed he had about the best rod and reel money could buy and felt that I had to impress him so I lied a bit.

"Of course I tie my own flies", I replied.

By this time I almost had the fish in.

He then asked, "What is the hardest fly that you have ever tied?"

I turned around and looked him square in the eyes.

"A mosquito with a one inch rope".

Well that guy didn't know what to think. He just stared at me as if I was half–crazy.

A couple of minutes later old Mr. Silversides had bit the dust. I had it cleaned and was about to cut the tail off when the American spoke up.

"I've read quite a bit about salmon fishing over the past winter but the books don't say anything about cutting the tails off. Why are you doing that?"

"I'm retailing salmon me boy – retailing salmon."

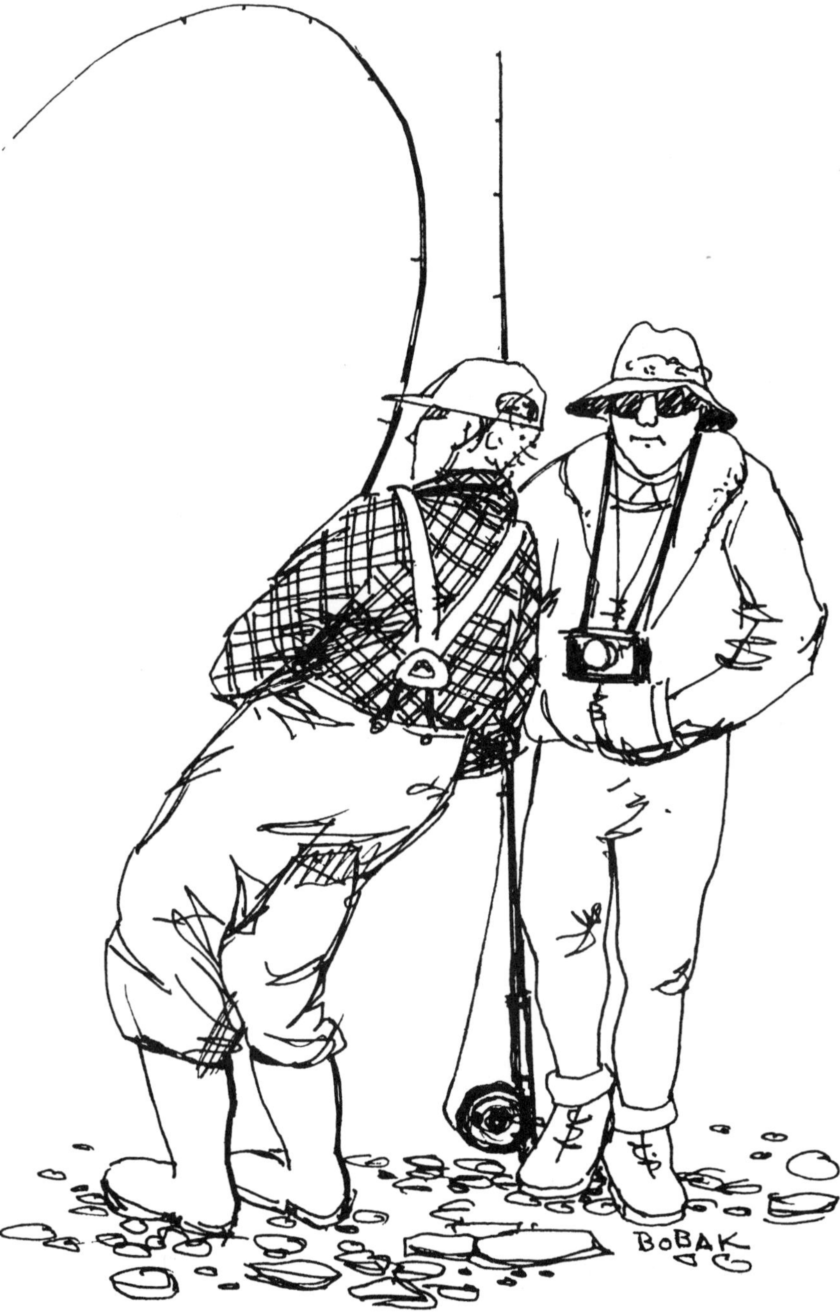
BOBAK

Well he took off mutterin' to himself and I could tell he was some kinda ugly. I heard through the grapevine that he said he run into a fisherman who was four bricks short of a load!

My First and Last Moose License

We were at our huntin' camp back of Boiestown. The other two lads was cookin' up breakfast so I said that I'd scout around for a moose. I had my brand new rifle with me and I sure felt lucky.

Dad always warned me to put the second bullet in 'em case they ain't truly dead. I thought about that as I was takin' a short run. I pulled out my birch–bark caller and gave a series of grunts and groans like you wouldn't believe. They musta worked because out strutted this big male moose with a giant set of antlers. I let him have it right in the heart and down he went. He looked dead as a door–nail as I walked up.

I laid my rifle across the antlers with the ring of the level on one of its points. I was preparin' to pull my hunting knife out of my sheath when up sprang the moose. Apparently I had only grazed it. Next thing ya know my coat got stuck in the antlers. Hello for goin'. He took off and we was clippin' right along at a good pace. There were a bunch of alders dead ahead and I knew somethun' was bound to happen. When we got through that mess I felt the top of my head and realized I'd gotten a brush–cut.

I knew that there was a beaver pond round there handy. By and by, we was headin' straight for it. He took off swimmin' and I was still with him. Before Mr. Bull Moose hit the opposite shore I climbed off and headed back to camp and told my companions what had transpired. They never believed a word I told them. I assured them that my rifle and coat were missing weren't they? – and I was soakin' wet wasn't I?

Well – to make a quick end to the story – the warden caught up with the moose about a week later. He charged the moose with leavin' the scene of an accident, carryin' stolen property and possession of a loaded fire–arm.

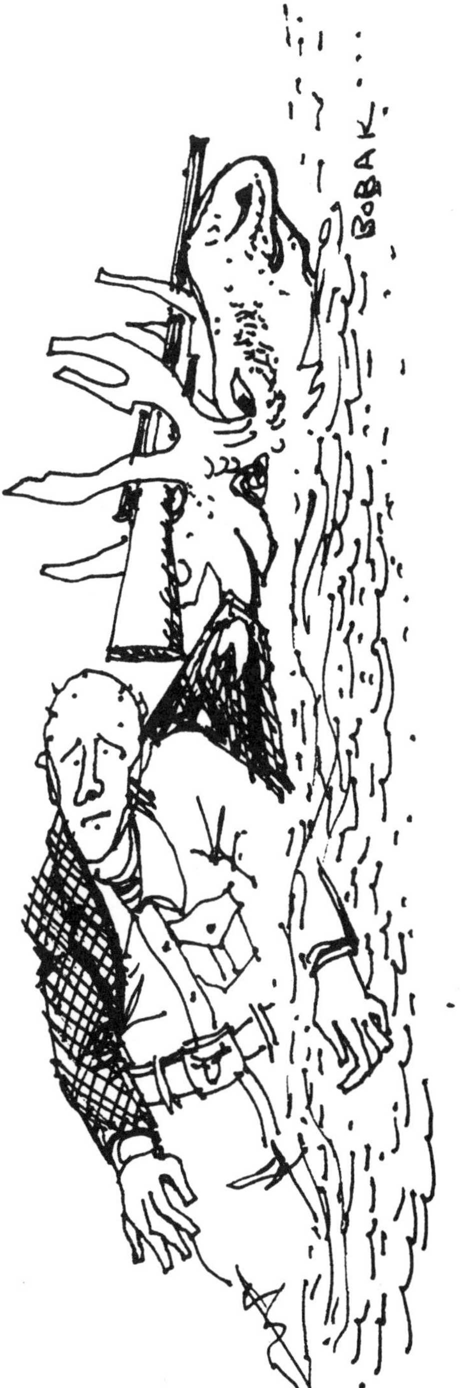
BOBAK

Fishin' for Trout

Fishin' today ain't nothun' like it used to be. I may not be the best trout fisherman in New Brunswick but I'm the second best. I've caught more of them there speckled trout than you could shake a stick at. I remember fishin' places where the fish was so thick I caught em' with a bare hook. In another spot I used to catch em' with my bare hands just for sport. I remember the time I was fishin' one of my secret honey–spots where you couldn't keep those 2–3 pound trout off your fly. Every cast you hooked a big one. I think that expression about 5 per cent of the fisherman catching 95 percent of the fish is right on the money. Ya know how some guys tell stories and lie through their teeth – geeze that bothers me. I reckon a person must have a certain amount of luck with their fishin'. They need a little patience and religion helps a mite too. Sometimes when things gets tough I take to recitin' this little verse called, "A Fisherman's Prayer".

> Lord give me grace
> To catch a fish so big
> That even when I, telling of it
> afterwards may never have to lie.

I always tell it like it is. Well – let me tell you about the time – oh about forty years ago now – that my father Alex and I was at our camp at the junction of Savage River and the Cains River. We drove in the yard – went to the bank of the river and spied the queerest thing. This here bear was walkin' towards the river with only three legs. We went into the camp and unloaded our riggin'. We sat down at the kitchen table and started chewin' the fat. Next thing ya know this sound of huffin' and puffin' was comin' from just outside the camp. We looked out and this four legged bear was headin' towards the over–turned molasses barrel. He reached one paw into the barrel and headed back to the river on three legs again. Well – when the bear got to the river it held out its paw with the molasses on it about 3 feet higher than the water. Pretty soon there was hundreds of flies, mosquitos and you name it flyin' around that bear's paw. In the meantime there were these big sea–trout jumpin' clean out of the water and ker–smash – he'd cuff 'em a good one. Then he'd heave em' up on to the shore. He had an awful rift of em'. They were nice fish – oh – about 2 to 6 pounders I'd say.

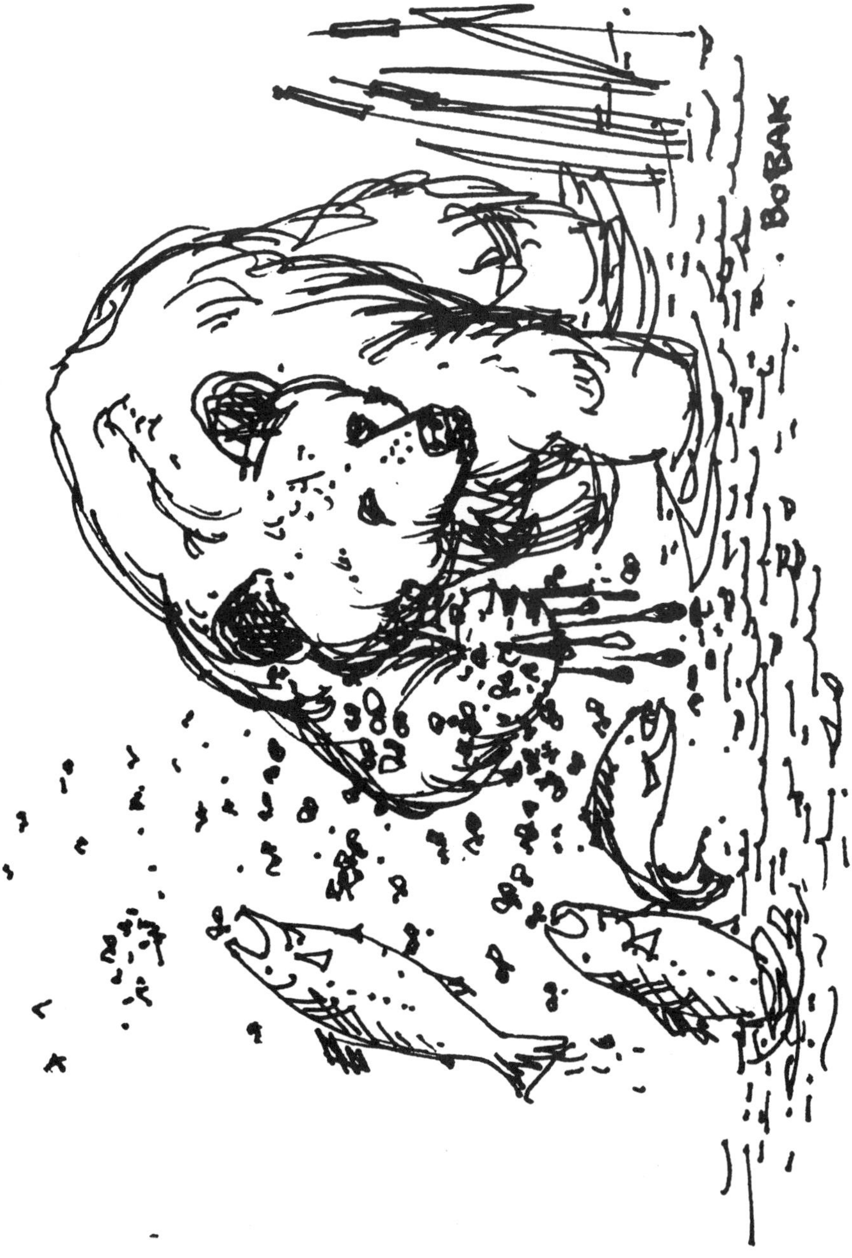
BOBAK

I made up my mind then and there that I wanted them there fish more than that dumb old bear. I had me an idea. I put a couple of slugs into my shot–gun and fired a couple of warnin' shots and that bear took off like a bolt of lightning. It was just like takin' candy from a baby. We ended up with our limits of sea–trout without wetting a line.

That was one humdinger of a story don't you think?

The Psychiatrist

One of John's regular customers decided to see a psychiatrist. It seems that he had just split up with his wife and was emotionally unstable. He also believed most of what John told him when he visited the shop.

It seems that throughout the session Johnny Washburn's name came up continually. The fellow told the psychiatrist things like Trudeau calling an election after two years in power, skeletons being found in the walls of the Barker House building, a bear driving John's truck, what happened to John when he was a prisoner in Vietnam, catching fish with the help of a bear, shooting a deer with a Vick's inhaler, etc.

The psychiatrist listened intently and documented the information. When the patient finished up the psychiatrist asked,

"Is that all?"

"Yes, I can't think of anything else right now. Is there any hope for me Doc? I gotta know."

"There's nothing wrong with you but when you see that Johnny Washburn, tell him I want to see him. I think he's the one that needs the professional help."

Somethun' Fishy

John Washburn was boardin' at Boiestown on the Miramichi when he was a lineman for N.B. Tel. The lady fed him fish cakes for breakfast, salt cod for dinner and salmon for supper. For a bedtime snack she gave him sardines and crackers. After two weeks with no change in the menu, John packed his suitcases one morning and got ready to leave.

When his hostess asked him,
"Where are you goin'?"
He answered, "I'm goin' upriver to spawn."

Free Money

One time John drilled holes in quarters and secured them in the sidewalk in front of his shop. Then he would spread a few pennies, nickels, and dimes amongst the twenty five cent pieces. When someone would come along John would tell everyone to come over to the window for a good laugh. Those trying to get the quarters would do just about anything to get them loose much to the delight of John and friends. One lady actually broke the heel right off her shoe. The police were called to quell the disturbance after receiving complaints over a period of time. John was told to cease operations.

The Time I Forgot My Rifle

Pat Delong drove me home from the barbershop around 2:00 in the afternoon so I could do a little huntin'. I changed into my huntin' clothes and when I went to get my .308 Caliber Remington rifle, I realized I'd left it in the trunk of the car my wife was driving.

That time of the season you could use slugs. I grabbed my 16 gauge pump–action shotgun and walked back onto the old truck road behind Silverwood. I shot my limit – 6 partridge using shot shells.

On my way back home this doe deer stepped out of the bushes and stood right in the middle of the road – broadside. When I reached for my slugs I realized I was out of luck because I had left them on the kitchen table.

I reckoned that I could figure out some way of getting that doe because I'm a pretty intelligent lad ya know. I reached into my coat pocket and felt for my Vicks inhaler. I dropped that down the barrel of the gun and squeezed the trigger. Down went the doe deer on the spot. When I went to field–dress the deer I smelled a strong aroma of Vicks. I never thought anything of it.

I took the deer to Norm Hachey's butcher shop on the Hanwell Road. He hanged it up for six days and then cut it up.

The day Norm cut the deer up the smell of Vicks fumes was prevalent throughout the shop. Some of the customers inquired if he was snuffin' Vicks or somethun' else. He said that he wasn't and that the smell must be comin' from the deer that John Washburn shot with his Vicks inhaler.

That winter my wife, relatives and neighbours and I spent a whole winter without the slightest symptom of the common cold.

My Haircut

One day I got my haircut from John. When I got home my wife said, "Where did you get that pathetic hair cut?"

I said "Johnny Washburn's."

She said, "Go back and tell him it is the worst mess I ever saw in my life!"

I went back and explained that my wife wasn't amused with my new haircut. She said not to come back until I got my hair looking half–civilized.

John said matter of factly,

"I musta got side–tracked that day Clarky. I told you many times before if anyone asked where you got your hair cut to tell em' Saint John didn't I? Well now you know why."

A Prisoner in Vietnam

Rollie Waddingham Sr. told me this story. It seems John got a little tight and landed on the steps of a good friend of his, waking the whole household up at 2 a.m. Well he put on quite a show. It seems he started cryin' and tellin' the couple of how he was captured and tortured in Vietnam. He went to extreme lengths to mention how he was beat with chains, had bamboo shoots placed under his fingernails and was even burned. John started to cry and the woman started to cry. She said that she understood why he might drink a little and that there was no shame in showing his emotions. They gave him a lunch and put him to bed. The next morning they fed him breakfast and he was on his way.

Well about a week later the friend ran into John's brother Bob. He said that it was a tragedy that happened to his brother in Vietnam wasn't it?

Bob said,

"What do you mean?"

The other fellow replied,

"I mean about how your brother John was captured, held prisoner of war and tortured in Vietnam."

Bob laughed, "John's never been out of the province in his life!"

The Doctor

I was at the Farmers' Market last Saturday mornin'. This lad was carryin' about 12 dozen eggs. It was rainin' somethun' fierce and the feller slipped and fell. The feller landed on his back and the eggs broke covering him from head to toe. He was shakin' like a leaf. It was an awful sight. Someone yelled "Get an ambulance." I said "Hold on a minute. I'm not a doctor but I think this lad is just shell–shocked."

The Surprise Election

Pat Delong and John Washburn caused quite a stir around Fredericton. Pat made a tape – there was some music, a Fredericton radio logo song, and then a special bulletin:

"We interrupt this program to bring you an important message. After only 2 years of being in power, Pierre Trudeau has called a surprise election." Then there was some more music.

Each time John had a customer in he'd play the tape which was hidden behind the radio. When it came to the part about a special bulletin John would head for the radio saying, "Let me turn that up – it sounds really important." After the message he'd shut the tape down and go on about Trudeau.

Well when the customers heard the news – they spread the word far and wide. John used to say that he had a north, south, east and west network in Fredericton and a few connections on the Miramichi. The patrons who knew John the least were the best messengers.

Johnny the Artist

One of John's customers came into the shop for a cut one day. As he sat down in the chair, John asked, "How would you like your hair cut today?" The customer replied, "John, I want you to leave my right side– burn on, cut the left – leave a bald spot on the back of my head, oh, the size of a 50 cent piece – make a bald spot on the left side, oh, the size of a 25 cent piece – make a couple of nicks on the right side – you know what I mean. Taper the left side in the back and square the right side. That should do the trick."

"Do you have any idea how you'll look with a mess like that?"

"Sure do. That's how you cut 'er the last time I was here."

"Well, that was a pretty unusual haircut I must say. Oh, by the way, do you remember if you tipped me anything extra for the art work?"

Johnny Washburn and the Barker House Skeletons

When they started to tear down the Barker House John got an idea. He would start a rumour that they had found some skeletons in the walls. He started off with a stranger whose hair he was cutting who enquired; "Who were those two distinguished gentlemen that just walked by with the fancy white fur coats?"

John thought for a moment and replied "Oh those guys. They are here investigating the skeletons they found when they started tearing that building down across the street. They're from the R.C.M.P. Crime Lab in Sackville."

Stranger: "I thought that there was somethun' different – somethun' peculiar."

John: You have got a good eye of judgin' character.

When the gentleman left John walked over to John Mitchell who was in charge of tearin' down the premises.

John Washburn: "I told a fellow that they found some skeletons between the walls. If anyone questions my story, will you go along with it?"

John Mitchell: "No problem John, you always had a knack for makin' up a story."

Well John told that yarn to his customers and even told a *Daily Gleaner* reporter who happened by. The reporter excitedly commented,

"Now that is the exact kind of story I'm lookin' for."

Everyone in Fredericton was talkin' about it, with stories of 2 to 6 skeletons being found. *The Daily Gleaner* had to publish a Disclaimer to put an end to all the phone calls it received. It was entitled "Just A Crazy Rumour".

Absolutely Unbelievable

My brother Bob and I were drivin' out this bull–dozed road back of the Hanwell Road. A buck deer ran across in front of the Dodge Ram 4 X 4. We stopped, grabbed our rifles and set out on foot after the deer. When we returned to where the truck had been parked, there was another truck, red in colour. Stupified, I asked the driver,

"Have you seen a white Dodge truck?"

To which he answered,

"Yah – it's up around the corner flipped up on its side. I think there's somethun' in it."

We went up to the vehicle. The truck was flipped over, on its side with the window still half open. There was a bear stuck inside, tearin' my truck all to pieces.

We sent the other fellah out to get the ranger with a tranquillizer gun.

After awhile, the ranger arrived followed by a Mountie.

After they tranquillized the bear we examined the inside of the vehicle. The bear had eaten our sandwiches and polished off the rest of our half–gallon of rum.

The Mountie said,

"Could I have a word with the owner of this vehicle?"

I said,

"That's me."

He took me aside and said that he could charge me with leaving the keys in the ignition.

I said, "Are you goin' to charge the bear with theft and impaired drivin'?"

The last we heard was that the bear is still up at Woolastook Park awaiting trial for his charges.

Maggie Jean Chestnut

As told by Eva Searle

The Maggie Jean Chestnut Residence represents a dream that began in 1911. It came true thirty-eight years later, in 1949. It involves people – Mrs. H.G. Chestnut and her daughter Maggie Jean, Lord Beaverbrook and Mr. Ashley Colter. Hundreds of others were involved.

Mrs. Chestnut was the first president of the UNB Alumnae Society when it was organized in 1911. The foremost thought of the members was to provide a residence for UNB girls who were away from home. Maggie Jean heard the chatter about the residence when she was a very small girl.

The ladies of the Alumnae Society held bridge parties, teas and concerts and the building fund grew very slowly. Maggie Jean heard about that, too.

The years passed.

In 1927 Maggie Jean went to UNB. Muriel Farris (later Mrs. R.D. Baird) was a classmate and they talked about the residence.

In 1948 Mrs. Baird became president of the Alumnae Society and the dream approached reality when the ladies saw just what they wanted. They had their eyes on the beautiful house at the corner of Charlotte and Church Streets in Fredericton. Lord Beaverbrook had bought it from the Bank of Montreal. So a letter went to His Lordship

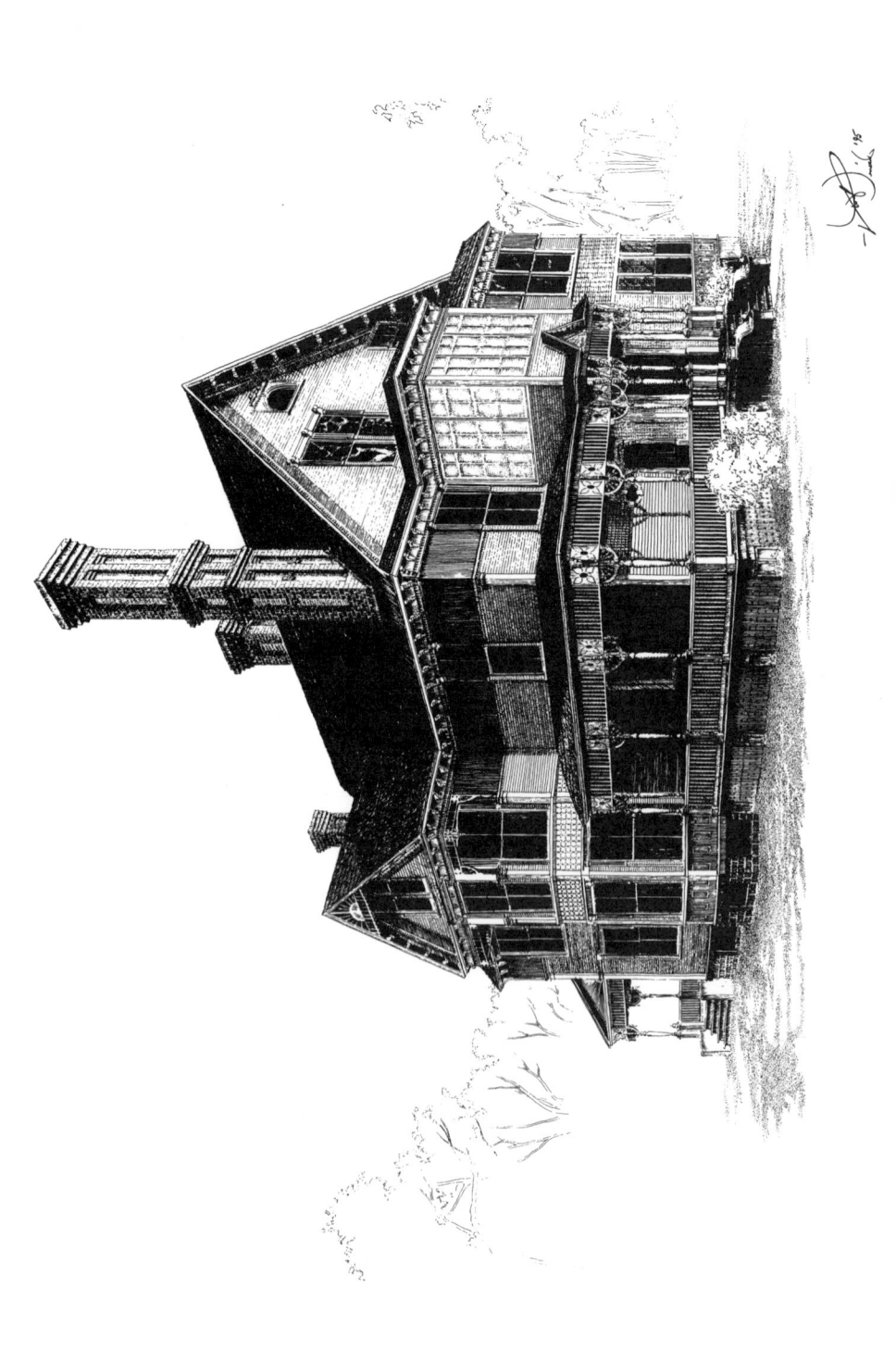

to tell him they would like to buy it and they mentioned the sum of money they had. It was very small. His Lordship was evasive.

The ladies persisted.

In April 1949 Lord Beaverbrook wrote Mrs. Baird a letter in which he said: "I offer the Bank of Montreal house to the Alumnae Society for use as a residence for women. I attach only one condition to the gift and that is that the society must now raise a sufficient sum of money to alter and equip the building for the intended use. I shall be glad to hear from you after you have consulted your colleagues. This offer runs out on December 31, 1949."

They had from April to December to raise an estimated $30,000. They could see no way. But Mr. Ashley Colter found a solution to the problem so they could accept the gift, and a plan was immediately put into action.

As Lord Beaverbrook expressed it – "It was a story of high endeavor, brilliantly directed and completely successful."

A residence board including Mrs. G.A. Addy, Mrs. C. McN. Steeves, Mrs. Coulter King, and Dr. Alice Sterling was struck. Later, others were appointed – Isabel Babbitt McKay, Margaret Phillips Brown, Shirley Pugh Weyman, Mary VanWart Morrison, Bernice Gunn and Myrtle Scott Hagerman. On a chilly October morning in 1949 the residence was opened with a coffee party. Lord Beaverbrook was there in his happiest mood, greeting those who had helped so faithfully.

Mrs. H.G. Chestnut was there. But Maggie Jean was no longer with them. She had died in February 1949.

Maggie Jean had known the house for many years. In fact, in her college days she had been initiated in the basement of the Bank of Montreal house. With the freshettes she bobbed for apples, ate arrowroot biscuits and drank water while the older students ate a delicious lunch upstairs in the dining room.

All her life Maggie Jean had been devoted to the university. She had been deeply involved in the fund raising for the Students Memorial Building and had been a member of the Senate.

On opening day in 1949 her classmates remembered her as she had climbed the hill on other frosty mornings proudly wearing her UNB jacket – a sturdy young student and fine sportswoman. The residence would bear her name.

The Maggie Jean Chestnut House has provided hundreds of young ladies from all over the world a "home away from home".

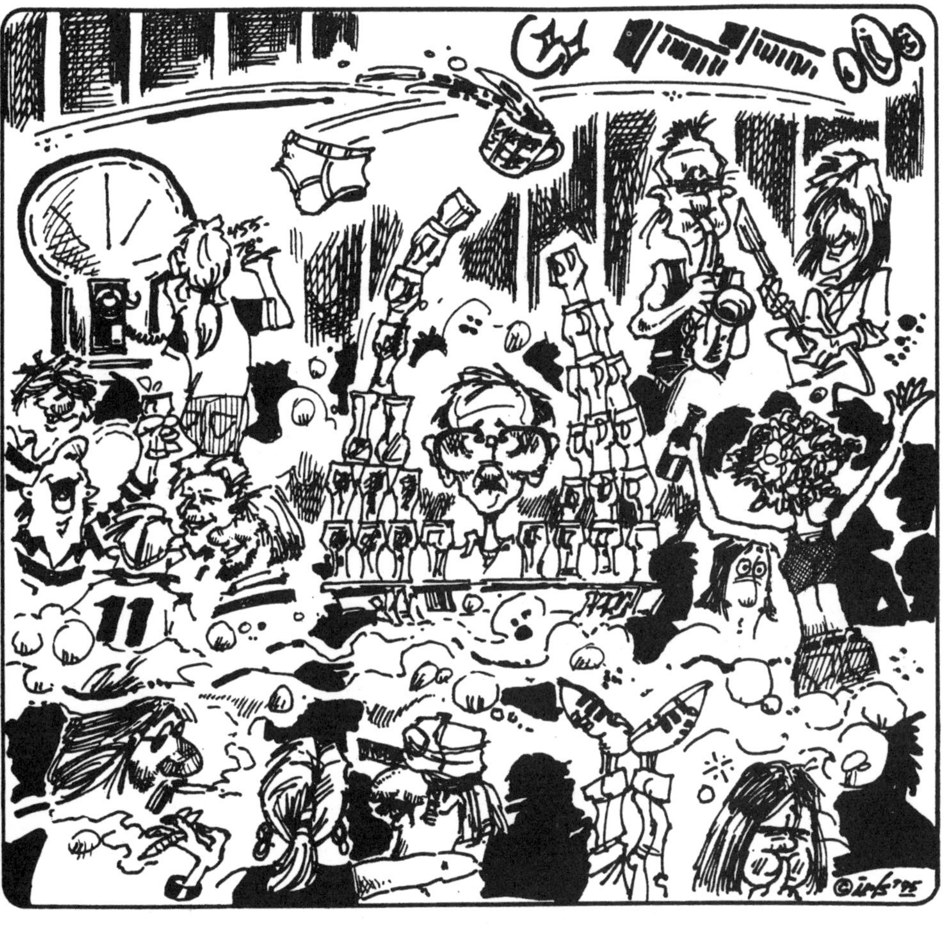
11

The Riverview Arms

The Riverview Arms Tavern was a Fredericton institution in the 1970s and was revered with near cult status by the "regulars". The Tavern was indeed a unique place to meet and greet old friends and to make new acquaintances.

The Riverview Arms opened in 1965 under the ownership of Larry Usler. The building itself was a historic structure, having been built in the 1850s on a piece of land on the banks of the Saint John River commonly referred to as the Salamanca Landing. Prior to becoming the Riverview Arms, the building had housed the Kent Inn which offered fine dining and facilities for banquets, weddings and other special functions. Many clients of the Inn fondly recall the elegant chandeliers that graced the ceilings. These had come directly from Government House.

From its beginnings, the Riverview Arms was unique and at the forefront in its field. From 1965 to 1969, for example, the Riverview Arms catered exclusively to men, but in 1969, the Arms became the first tavern in New Brunswick to allow women accompanied by a male escort. Indeed, at the time, the sign outside the tavern read "Ladies and Escorts". In 1973 the tavern was opened to both sexes of legal drinking age and the business really began to flourish.

The Arms had few set rules with the exception of the enforcement of the legal drinking age, nineteen years since 1972, and restrictions related to damage to property. Otherwise, the rules were pretty lax, and this state of affairs appealed to the Arms' customers. It was a known fact, for example, that something stronger than cigarettes could be smoked on the premises, and it was not an uncommon sight to see individuals dancing on table tops in the wee small hours of the morning. Indeed, the Arms could be described as "wild and woolly" at times. Customers came to have a good time and rarely left disappointed.

In the early 1970s, one entertainer named Wetzel put on quite a show. Paid to play guitar and sing, one of his favourite songs was called "The Crystal Chandeliers". Wetzel would buy a few beers, the customers would buy him a few, and, almost on cue, not long before closing time, he'd tumble off his stool while performing. This was the highlight of the evening for many of the clients. At that time, streakers were getting a lot of attention in the media, and, of course, a few showed up at the Riverview Arms, to the astonishment of all present!

As for food, it was good and the prices were right. How about a steak and fries with a dill pickle served on a wooden platter for 99¢? The Arms' Saturday night suppers reflected New Brunswich cuisine at its best and cheapest: a free buffet of beans, weiners, brown bread, cole slaw and the works. And on Christmas Eve, free beer was offered the Arms' patrons. It goes without saying that the Arms' management and staff knew how to treat their valued customers.

How busy was the Arms you might wonder. According to NBLCC standards the seating capacity was 264 but on a busy night there were upwards of 350 customers packed in like sardines. The patrons came from all walks of life: doctors, lawyers, professors, blue–collar workers, teachers, and, of course, students could be found there on any given evening. Premier Hatfield stopped by from time to time and on one occasion, in the mid–1970s, the Prince of Wales paid a visit to the Arms.

Head waiter Art Blizzard recalls the Prince's visit as if it were yesterday. He received a call from a British officer in training at Camp Gagetown saying that Prince Charles and two bus–loads of soldiers would be arriving shortly, but not to worry, there would be no problems. The Brits came and took over the establishment. They had a great time, drinking and singing army songs. After a few hours, all 60 of them formed a line and marched out single file on their knees, each placing his left hand on the fellow's shoulder in front, chanting all the while. Art said that it was one of the funniest spectacles he had ever witnessed. He laughed so hard he cried.

Art relates another time in 1976 when the company supplying special NBLCC glasses was on strike. The owner, Larry Usler, gave Art $500 with orders to get back some of the glasses usurped by students. He went up to the University and put the word out that he would offer a 10¢ reward for each glass returned, no questions asked. Glasses came out of the wood-work. They brought them back in shopping bags, in gym bags, and by the trunk load. Even a couple of chairs and a table showed up!

In the mid-1970s the Riverview Arms was the busiest tavern east of Montreal with over 100 kegs sold weekly with a high of 110. That's 100 times 222 glasses of 9 oz draught, plus bottled beer, plus wine, an incredible amount of booze.

Speaking of records, Art sold 13 kegs, 12 flats, and a case of wine in a 12- hour shift in 1975, a Canadian record for a single bartender. Another waiter at the time, Bruce Lewis, recollects what happened to make that day so busy.

"It was the last day of classes at UNB and there was a major snowstorm. The Hilltop closed early but we stayed open. We quite literally got swamped! We sold 35 kegs of beer that day."

Indeed, the Riverview Arms was never intimidated by foul weather. On another occasion, its doors remained open in spite of a general power failure and bottled beer was served by candle light.

The Riverview Arms had all kinds of gimmicks to attract the customers' attention. There was always green beer sold on St. Patrick's Day. There was birthday beer and special prices on draught, sports teams were treated with free beer on occasion, and Hallowe'en contests were organized. Events such as Auction 45's tournaments, a "New Wave" night and a "Reggae" night, to name a few, proved popular.

The "Miramichi Revival" day, an annual ritual, warrants special attention. On March 8, 1980, for example, a total of 31 kegs of beer were sold by three waiters. The doors were locked at 9:30 am, the place being already crowded to capacity. What a zoo! The Miramichiers invaded Fredericton, bolstered up with UNB and St. Thomas students from the area. They arrived with their guitars and fiddles and mouth organs, and everything else they needed for a rootin' tootin' party Miramichi style. The Arms supplied the beer, of course. They rocked the place, morning, noon and night, but in spite of all the beer consumed, there were very few problems. No one wanted to get barred!

That evening around 9:00 p.m. Mike Sears and I went down to the basement to see how the floor was holding up on the band side. We were aghast to see that the floor was heaving up and down under the weight of the revellers upstairs. We just looked at each other and shook our heads. Mike said, "If it was going to go by now, it would have."

Besides the "Miramichiers", many men's and women's rugby teams frequented the Riverview Arms. I think they came to their watering hole to quench their thirst, of course, but also to heal their bodies. After a few beers, their aches and pains subsided. It was nothing to have six to eight teams consisting of The Exiles, The Loyalists, the UNB Ironmen, the STU Tommies, the Saint John Trojans, the Moncton Marshawks, the Oromocto Pioneers, and the Kings County Lions, all crowded into the tavern in their rugby garb. Fierce competitors during the match, they were all comrades once they arrived at the Arms. They put on quite a show, joining in chug–a–lug songs, action packed songs such as "Sing High, Sing Low, Sweet Chario...", "Old MacDonald's Farm", "If I were the Marryin' Kind", to name a few. The song that became infamous at the Arms, and a theme song during rugby season, was one entitled "The Zulu Warrior". An individual, usually one of the male persuasion, would volunteer or be chosen to make a spectacle of himself. To the chants of "haul 'em down, you mighty warrior, haul 'em down, you mighty chief, chief", the individual would progressively remove an article of clothing until he was wearing nothing more than his birthday suit. Where else would one behold such a sight!!Besides events organized by the management, the Arms' customers often initiated their own reasons for coming: wakes, birthday parties, pre–game football warm–up parties, last–day of classes, and stag parties. Often when people planned on going out on the town or to a house party, the Arms was the natural starting point. If individuals wanted to talk or socialize or watch a hockey game, they gathered in the old section, whereas the rock an' rollers tended to frequent the newer section of the tavern.

Clients were well entertained by piped–in music or by live bands, some of the most popular of which were The Freightliners, Red Eye, Mad Hash, High Street, The Parts, Ernie Smith and Carlene Davis, and Howard Brook.

And to ensure that the service was top–notch, the Arms boasted some excellent waiters in the '70s, including Art Blizzard, whom you've already met, Stella Harvey, John Zimmerman, Harold McGrath, Bruce Lewis, Pat Buckley, Ron Clark, Dave Cochrane, Ron Trimball, Tim Dow, and Mike Sears, to name a few. These professionals had to deal with their share of characters, guys with handles such as Spider, Monkey, Hoss, Roo–roo, Nar, Dogan, Herb, Fakey, Arty, Cat, Happy, Smitty, Toad, Fiji, Dicker, Bear, Gig the Pig, Bushman and Mad Dog, a personality to behold. An electrician by trade, and usually pretty flush, Mad Dog would saunter in and have a few with his friends. What a transformation! From a Dr. Jekyll, he would turn into a Mr. Hyde. A little tight, he would grit his teeth, growl, and bark like a dog! If you didn't understand what was going on, you would declare he was a case for the looney bin!

How did I come into the Riverview Arms? Well, I was interviewed by a man–of–the–cloth, would you believe? He related to me the parable in which Diogenes entered a village, carrying a lit lantern in the middle of the day. People approached him and asked him what he was doing, to which he responded, "I'm looking for an honest man". "Well, Mr. Clark," my interviewer commented, "we're looking for an honest man and we feel you fit the description. Do you want the job as manager?" I agreed, and there I stayed for a year.

They were very few dull moments. I was told when I was first employed that anything that isn't nailed down risks being stolen, including our glasses, fire extinguishers, tables, chairs, etc. One night a customer told Art and me that some guy was stealing a chair out the back door. We soon caught up with him. Art yelled, "Put the chair down, son", coming across with a "love tap" to the jaw that knocked him down. "Let me see you try to steal that." Art had a unique sense of humour in dealing with situations like that. He was a great guy to work with.

Merv Burchill was the manager and then owner of the Arms in the '80's. In June 1989, economics forced the Arms to close its doors forever and one of the greatest taverns of all time passed into history. The Riverview Arms lives but as a memory. It will always hold a special place in my heart.

"The Bear Man"

Everyone has heard of characters such as Frankenstein, The Wolfman, Dracula, the Hunchback from Notre Dame etc. Did you know that there actually existed a person – half–man and half–bear in New Brunswick? Some say that his last name was Mersereau. He was born in a place called Iron Bound Cove, near Chipman, around 1850.

The story tells us that the Bear–man's father was not what you would call an intelligent sort by any means of the imagination. He and his wife lived in a hovel and were extremely poor. One day while out hunting he shot a bear, cleaned it and transported the carcass back to his homestead. He propped the bear up against the door and knocked. When his pregnant wife opened the door she fell over backwards from the weight of the bear which landed on top of her. This sounds like an old wive's tale but so goes the story. When the baby was born he exhibited bear–like characteristics.

Bruce Wallace, an elderly gent from Chipman, recollects the story his mother told him of this thing – half bear and half man that showed up regularly in the school yard begging for food. The kids welcomed the "Bear–Man" and he would affectionately give each and every one a little bear–hug. The kids thought he was a great friend. When pressed for time he'd get down on all fours and go like the Devil. He could outrun all of the kids. He was often seen herding cows like a trained dog and catching fish with his bare hands.

Another gentleman from the community, Fred Davidson, remembers clearly what his mother told him. She described the "Bear Man" as "some kinda spectacle to behold." He seldom stayed home but preferred to roam the country-side. He couldn't speak but it is rumoured that his parents could understand him to a degree. He was frequently seen travelling from Gaspereau to Midland, all the while begging for food. He wouldn't set foot on a bridge but preferred to swim or wade across. One of the schools where he used to hang out was Gaspereau School. There was a sheep farm nearby. The "Bear-Man" would get down on all fours and chase the sheep all over the place. The kids would reward him by sharing their apples, sandwiches and cookies. Fred also remembered his mother telling him that when the "Bear-Man" walked it would appear as if he had drunk one too many.

The photo is a copy of an original taken in the San Francisco area. Eldon Robichaud in Moncton wrote to me saying that his mother-in-law got the picture when she was a young girl around 1930.

Some rumours suggest that the parents sold him to the P.T. Barnum Circus. It is a fact that he performed in the freak show. He travelled all over the United States and the rest of the world.

The circus was travelling on a showboat and the "Bear-Man" made a fatal mistake of grabbing a young lady and giving her a friendly bear-hug. She freaked out and screamed. Back in the 1800's many of the men brandished pistols for self-protection. Her husband ran to the rescue and fearing for his wife's safety shot and killed the "Bear-Man". The papers at the time carried a head-line stating "A Tragic Ending for the Kind and Gentle Bear-Man."

Henry Braithwaite

By 1900 Henry's name was already famous among international moosehunters from the United States, England, France and many other places throughout the world. He was the man who put New Brunswick on the map as a big game hunter's haven, as well as initiating the guiding trade.

Braithwaite was born in Fredericton on January 12, 1840. At an early age he moved to the Penniac area. It was there that he met an Indian Maliseet Chief, Gabriel Echkewen or "Sachem Gabe". The Chief usually stopped at the Braithwaite's residence on the way to and from his hunting trips. He taught Henry a great deal about the birds, animals and fish that inhabited the forest and streams. He also taught Henry about the Indian way of life in the woods.

By the time Henry was 12 he was accompanying "Sachem Gabe" on hunting trips. At the age of 13 Henry shot his first caribou. He was destined to become New Brunswick's big game hunter and first white guide. He tried lumbering for a while but lost some money and gave it up forever. He loved the woods. He would take his essentials and head to the far reaches of the Miramichi. After a while he developed a pattern. In the fall he would hunt moose and caribou, trap fur–bearing animals all winter and shoot bears in the spring. And then the cycle would repeat itself.

As he grew older, Henry began his career as a guide. In those days the hunters lived in tents – a rugged ordeal for many rich men not

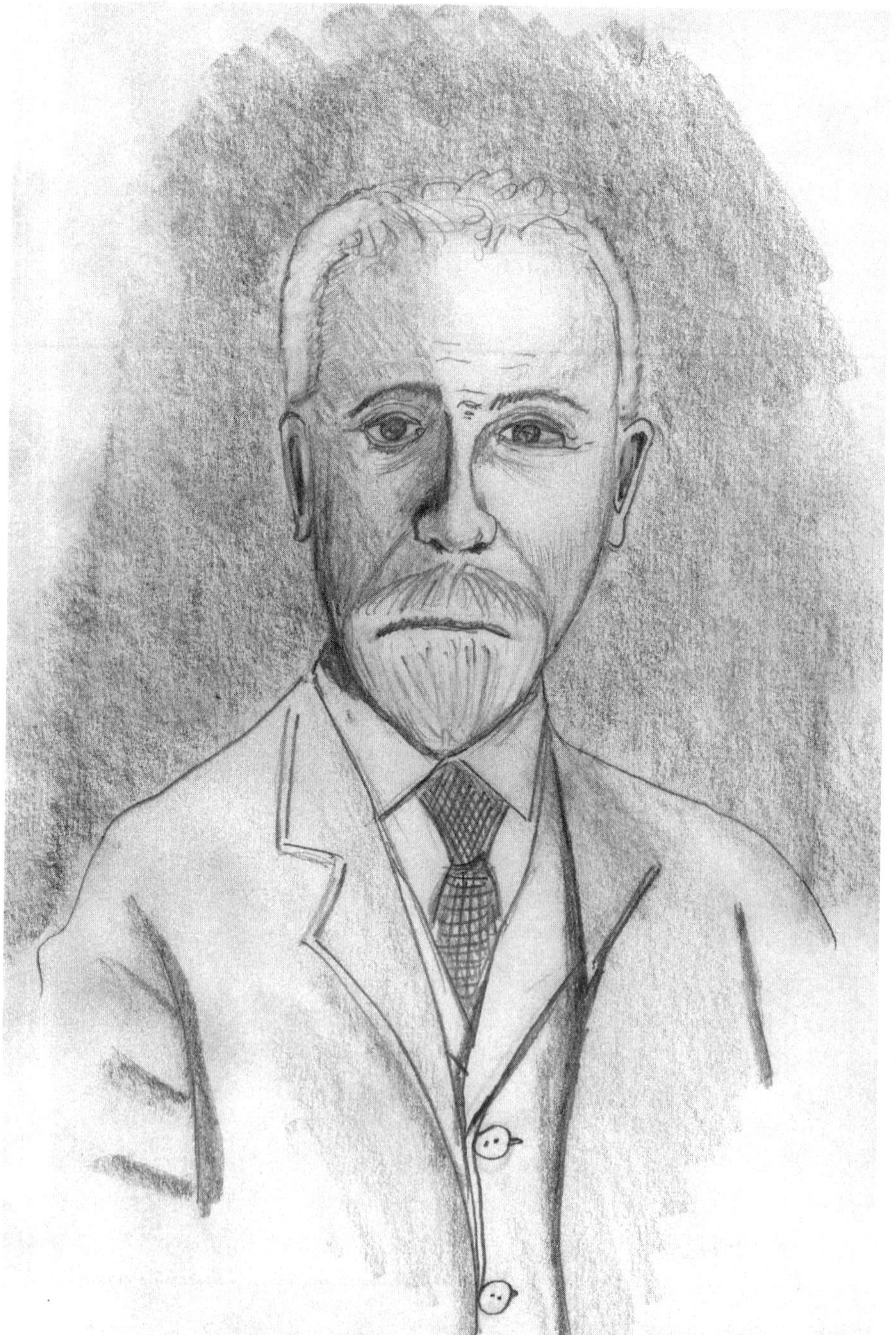
R Bailey

accustomed to "roughing it". Henry was the first man to build primitive log camps. Once he started guiding parties of big game hunters for moose heads "Uncle Henry" was never to be unemployed again. At one particular time he had twenty some camps and lean–tos throughout New Brunswick – some were up to seventy–five miles and four to five days from the nearest town.

Henry's fame grew so much that a lake and a mountain were named after him. Indeed, one sport claimed that he tried for over 10 years to hire the services of Henry. He was booked by his agent three years ahead. No guide in the world was as popular.

Some say that he would go into a trance–like state and could actually communicate with the animals of the woods. One fact is certain – he knew the woods and animals like the back of his hand. He was a rugged individual make no mistake. Once he broke his kneecap in three places. Somehow he dragged his bad leg nine miles to camp, cut a branch and trekked forty miles to the nearest settlement. Think about it!

The following is one of Henry's bear stories that was published in the Family Herald and Weekly Star of Montreal for April 13, 1924.

I came to a camp one night and found that a bear had been around that day and eaten some rotten meat that had been thrown out. I had brought fresh bait with me, but it was too late to set the trap, and thinking the bear might come again that night, I set a rifle and rigged a purchase so he would shoot himself.

I had been wearing a pair of untanned moose shanks, and as the warm weather was making them smell badly, I left them outside the camp door when I took them off. I lay awake until nearly midnight waiting for the gun to go off but heard nothing. When I woke in the morning I found the bear had walked past the trap to the door and had taken the moccasins. I had to walk eight miles in my stocking feet to get another pair. Before starting I set the trap and left it but the bear never came back. Perhaps the moccasins killed him.

Henry Braithwaite died in his sleep at his home in Fredericton on January 30, 1927, a legend in his own time.

My Biggest Trout

as told by Charlie Clayton

Back about 1925 I used to sell a few trout. You'd go down to the Penniac and you'd have all you wanted. I remember one time when my mother said, "Don't stay too long", cause she was gettin' dinner ready. My brother and I was just young fellahs. We wasn't down there too long – we got 8 or 10 and she cooked them on a baker's sheet She cut the head and tail off and 7 of em' would fill that cookie sheet. She'd cook em' with a layer of bacon on 'em. Boy they tasted great.

Trout didn't mean anything. Oh yah – there was all kinds of trout, you'd go down to the stream and you'd see them in bunches in the pools. They'd be full of em'.

The biggest trout I ever caught – I caught it on a bare hook – nothin else – just the hook. To tell you the truth I was goin' to catch it illegal. I saw the fish plain as day. I thought – I'll jig the lad – if I can. I put the hook in the water – it went down – and that fish swam right over and took a hold of it and bit it. It was quite a little while before I landed it. It weighed 3 pounds. It was the biggest one I ever got. Years ago – when I was a kid – they were all big trout.

37

Do Bright Salmon Ever Eat?

According to expert anglers and biologists alike ascending salmon in summer and fall do not eat. Well we all know that salmon are one of the most unpredictable game fish in the world – ask any angler. Ernie Hall told me a story about what happened to his brother Louis and his sports. Louis guided and outfitted for 39 years of his life so he knew a bit about fishing. Here is his story.

"My brother Louis was up the Little Southwest. The camp was on a side hill and there was a big ledge down below where the bridge crossed the river. He had Dr. Turner, Dr. Ross Wright and I believe Dr. Reed with him. Doc Reed did the cookin'. They were up on the ledge lookin' down. There was a lot of those – some people call them fresh water shrimp – floatin' around. They look like a little lobster – a crayfish of some kind.

Down at the lower end of the pool there was some slick water. We could look in and see 3 big salmon layin' there – in about 4 feet of water. One of those shrimp went by – it was 3 inches long. It went right down beside these salmon, right by the tail of the biggest one. He wheeled and swung and caught it. They watched for a while and he never spit it out.

Louis' sports hooked and landed some nice salmon and when they dressed their fish, they discovered salmon with 3 and 4 of those shrimp inside. Some of them were pretty nearly all digested – some of them partly – and some of them fresh from just being swallowed. Those fish

39

appeared to be eatin', wouldn't you say?

To back up this story, my neighbor Ernie Scott, who has fished salmon for over 30 years, recalled a similar incident.

"I was fishin' at my camp on the Miramichi around the middle of June when I hooked a nice salmon. I brought it to shore and there were 5 smelt in it – 2 of them were half–digested.

In 1981 up the St. John River there was a mass infestation of army worms and millions of them were floating down the river. I heard reliable reports from anglers that some of the salmon were full of those.

Jack Fenety recalls fishing at the Church Pool on the Nashwaak in July of 1975. He hooked and landed a good–sized grilse around 5 pounds. He said that when he got home and cleaned the fish it had a salmon parr inside. Apparently the grilse swallowed the parr tail–first. Jack said that maybe the parr was botherin' the grilse – God only knows.

Check the inside of the next salmon you catch – who knows what you might find!

Dry Fly Fishing

told by Ernie Hall

It's a lot of fun fishing dry fly. I went up to Hartt's pool one time and the old feller was sittin' there in the yard. He said,
"Where do you think you're goin'?"
I said, "I'm goin' down to catch myself a salmon."
"There hasn't been a fish taken here in eight days. The water temperature is 80 degrees."
I told the gentleman of my intentions of trying dry fly. Well I went down and I put on a dry fly – I was fishing just off "Slaughter–house bar" where we used to land the fish. I dropped the anchor in the boat and started fishin' away.
I had these fish – I knew they were grilse comin' up all around the canoe.
There was another feller that came along and he was watchin' me and talkin' to the old feller. I heard the new fellah say,
"Who's that standin' up in the canoe"?
The old feller said, "That's that crazy fool Ernie Hall – thinks he's goin' to catch a fish – ya know he's crazier than a bag of hammers." The old feller forgot that the sound carried awful nice along the water. I could hear them plain as day. The guy was Jeff Richards. He came down and asked if I was havin' any luck. I said "Watch this."

I had one comin' on each side and one below the canoe. The water was nice for dry–fly fishing. I cast out to the left and this fish came up and took a crack at er' and missed it. I dropped it down in the front of the canoe and let the fly float down. This thing came up and took a look at it and one over on the right. The feller right below seemed to be the most interested. I dried the fly off good and cast below and this fish come up and inhaled the fly. I got that one.

Well – there was a stump hooked onto the bar. There was quite a roll every now and again. I lifted the anchor and I dropped down so I could get a good cast. I had a very light leader on. I thought I saw a slight boil so I cast my fly towards the spot. He came up and took quite a crack at it. I waited a few minutes and dropped it out there again. This time he really grabbed it. He just took one run and as far as I know he's still goin'. He had my leader and fly with him. That thing looked like a pig when he came out of the water after that fly. My God it was a big fish.

Levi Grant

Few men alive know the woods any better than Levi Grant who resides on the outskirts of Juniper. Levi was born at Cloverdale in August, 1925. At the age of 10 Levi spent the summer at the forks of the Miramichi at his father's camp. This is where he learned to pole a canoe.

"Bert Lyons was a fish warden there", Levi recalls. "He had a big wooden boat – 20 feet long. He didn't do much riverin'. I used to go up there and bail his boat out. He asked me if I could pole it. He told me to help myself. I poled that boat up and down the south branch. I hung right with it so I could pole on one side and steer around the rocks. That's how I learned to pole."

At the age of 13 Levi left school after grade six and took out a guide's license. He weighed 90 pounds at the time. His first customer was none other than the famous Woodstock author, historian, fisherman, archeologist and dentist, Dr. George Frederick Clarke. Levi remembered a trip to Boiestown that year. The water was too high to navigate downriver from Boiestown so they drove down by car. A fellah by the name of Calhoun where they stayed that night asked George how long he would be on the river. He told him about two weeks and that he was looking for Indian relics. He said that they planned on going up to Big Clearwater. The fellah said "Where's your guide? George motioned over to Levi. The fellah said that he might be able to pole up there in 2 weeks. As it turned out Levi had George up there in a day and a half!

Levi went to work in the woods in 1940. He knows what it is like to go to work in the morning by lantern and to come home by lantern. When he wasn't lumbering he was honing his hunting and trapping skills. Under his father's tutelage, he also became an expert craftsman of ash baskets, fishing creels, clothes hampers and even large pack baskets. He has never advertised but has a constant supply of customers. He says that he has a hard time keeping up. In the winter time he enjoys his hobbies, along with trapping.

New Brunswick woods stories always sooner or later come back to the cougar, that elusive and mysterious creature that haunts the mind of every New Brunswicker who loves the outdoors.

By the late 1800s, thanks to man, the eastern panther, a close relative of the western cougar, was gone from eastern Canada, or at least that's what the experts think. Nevertheless, there have always been stories of individuals encountering or sighting the ghost of North America. Levi's story is one of them ... "Oh, I was just out huntin' in early November. It had snowed about an inch but there was no snow on the ground – just on the trees. I went up to the ridge. I was still in the soft woods – there was no big trees – just a lot of little ones. I heard this thing holler. It let out a deadly yell that would have woken up the dead. I let a big whoop out of me and it answered. I rolled a cigarette and let another whoop out of me and it answered again. It was handier by that time. Then I could hear him – plain as day – comin' down the ridge – crunch, crunch, crunch – I could hear him jumpin' comin' down the hill as he was hittin' the leaves. I couldn't see standin' up so I sat against a big birch and waited. I could see about 60 feet in front of me. I was all ready – sittin', waitin', waitin'. He was comin' straight for me. All at once the noise stopped. When he hit the soft wood – you couldn't hear him – there was no frozen leaves. All at once he let this deadly yell out of him right behind me – about a hundred feet away. He went right around me and when he struck my tracks he let a yell out of him. My hat come right up on the top of my head – I went right in the air too. I looked at all four sides at once but I couldn't see nothun'. I heard him hit the hardwood ridge again – he hit the leaves. When I got out to him he was just cappin' the top of the hill. I was on about a 45 degree angle when I saw him goin' up that there tree. He was fawn in colour with a long tail – weighed maybe 150 pounds. When I got up to where I spotted him I saw his set of tracks. Each track

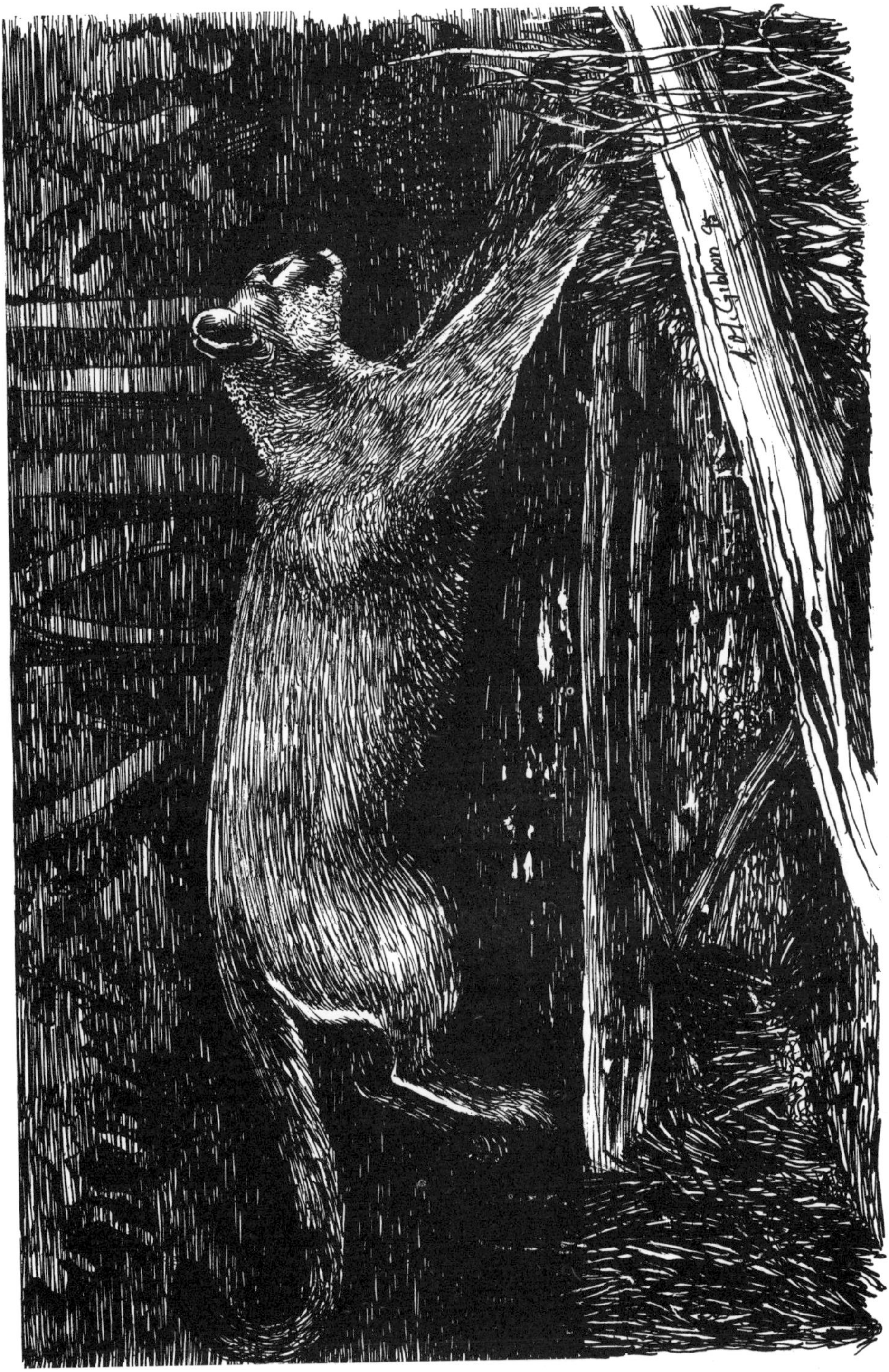

was about 4 1/2 inches wide and about 12–15 feet apart on the uphill. He went up a tree and musta went from one tree to another. I found his tracks about 300 feet away."

In 1992, Levi's story got a boost of credibility when he was involved in the first official documentation of a cougar's presence in New Brunswick since 1938. On November 16th, he received a phone call from a friend, Lewis Stone. Lewis told him that he had come across some fresh cougar tracks at Deersdale. Levi told him that he had seen some tracks himself about a week ago. They decided to call the Department of Natural Resources. Biologists Jeff Dempsey and Rod Cumberland accompanied Levi and Lewis for two miles. In one place one of the biologists found a scat sample and put it in his pocket. In another place there was a limb a good 20 inches off the ground. The animal had stepped over that and never left a mark. Levi said to the others:

"He's got quite long legs doesn't he?" They went down to another place – a little skidder trail. The fir trees were only three and four feet high. The cat cleared the clump of trees a distance of a good 5 metres without knocking any of the snow off the bushes. The biologist did a measurement of the distance that cat had leaped – 5.25 metres!

The following is an excerpt from "The Canadian Field – Naturalist." Cumberland, Roderick E., and Jeffrey A. Dempsey. 1994. Recent confirmation of a Cougar, Felis concolor, in New Brunswick. Canadian Field –Naturalist 108 (2): 224–226.

The presence of Cougar (Felis concolor) in the northeast, specifically New Brunswick, has been a controversial topic for decades, due primarily to an abundance of reports and sightings confounded by a lack of physical evidence. However, on 16 November, 1992, characteristics and measurements of tracks and identification of hair from a cat found near Deersdale, New Brunswick were determined to be that of a Cougar. Confirmation of the endangered subspecies, the eastern Cougar (Felis concolor couguar) is not possible with the collected data.

Key Words: Cougar, Felis concolor, Eastern Cougar, F.c. couguar, New Brunswick.

Levi has worked for J.D. Irving Ltd. for the past 17 years from May 15 to September 15 as a warden. Few could match his skill at handling a 26 foot boat and motor. During the month of June, Levi patrols daily the North branch above Juniper including Beadle Brook. This is an extremely rugged river section with huge boulders, lots of rapids and winding curves. Some places the water is only three inches deep. Levi claims that he can go up or down that section night or day.

Levi laughingly relates that he is one of the few who can dictate to the Irvings what they can and cannot do. The Irvings have an exclusive holding on Beadle Brook and Levi often guides the Irving brothers, Arthur and Jim. Levi allows only two trout a day retention when the normal limit is five. Arthur once landed an 8 pound brook trout there.

Levi at 70 is still going strong – patrolling the lakes and rivers for J.D. Irving in the spring and summer. In the winter time he continues to trap and fashion hand–crafted baskets.

The Bear Story

as told by George McDonald

This is a true story that happened to me October 15, 1980 at night. I was workin' buildin' a barn and it got dark so I went into my house to get a cup of tea. I wasn't overly tired and decided to take a bed out to the huntin' camp. My youngest daughter was 11 and she wanted to come. I said no, that I was takin' the huntin' dog and would only be a few minutes.

Anyways I finished my tea and the dog and I left. I was carryin' this single bed on my shoulder – it wasn't too heavy. I had a flashlight but I didn't have it on. I got pretty good night vision – I got lots of practice travellin' at night.

The Sunday before, I had been out in the daylight and saw a doe and two lambs and a porcupine in the same area. As we went down onto my last field I heard this runnin'. My dog Jake started barkin'. He ran and I called him. As I got close to the spruce tree I heard some scratchin' so I laid my bed down. This was the same tree that we cut the limbs off so we could hunt out of it. I put the light up the tree and of course the porcupine or what I thought was the porcupine was way up the tree. I was about to leave when I heard a deafening roar. The dog was still barkin'. I had the flashlight on and I looked and there was a female bear. I didn't know it at the time. She walked in under the snake–rail fence. She wasn't runnin' but she was walkin' steady. I didn't know what to do – run or I could climb the tree.

I had the light on her and hollered at her but she never let up. I thought my best bet was to go up the tree. I probably got up 10 feet when I heard her hittin' the tree. Fortunately for me she didn't follow me but I don't know why. I was goin' up through good goin' – the limbs had been cut out and I could go quite fast. When a person is terrified, you can go pretty fast. Next thing you know she was drawin' a bead straight up for me. She tried to get me 2 of 3 times when I was goin' up the tree. When I got up to where we normally sat at 25 feet – she was still comin' at me. I had to go higher. I got up another 15 feet and I shined the light up to where there was a crow's nest up on top.

I saw another bear up there and it looked awful big. It wouldn't matter big or not – I wasn't goin' to touch it. It dawned on me after a while it must be a cub. The cub was about 10 feet away from me.

I stepped down on one limb and the mother's brown nose reached through the limbs and caught me on the ankle. Fortunately I was wearing a rubber boot. She just ripped the boot and left her teeth marks in my ankle. I dropped the light. I was about 40 feet up by this time.

I knew there was a hemlock about 11 feet away – I knew it was there. I walked out and dove for the hemlock and went down about 10 feet. Needless to say I fetched up. A limb went through my cheek and I had to have 3 stitches in it. I cut my tongue but they didn't have to put stitches in it.

When I landed in the tree – I just kicked the broken limbs off. I didn't say anything – she knew I was there. I thought if I could get it settled down and if I could get the dog from barkin' – I could go home.

The bear went down the tree. Jake barked at her and she growled but the worst of it all was the grindin' of her teeth which I never heard before. That wasn't pleasant. When they are mad they can really grind.

About 5 minutes later – I had picked out my escape route just in case. I couldn't go to the next tree over which was a cedar in case I had to get back. I figured that she would bring the cub out. Anyways, I could see the lights in my house. I could see them walkin' in my kitchen about a third of a mile away. I couldn't identify who was there. I could see through the patio doors and I could see them walkin' in the kitchen.

Eventually the dog stopped barkin' which was a good sign. In a

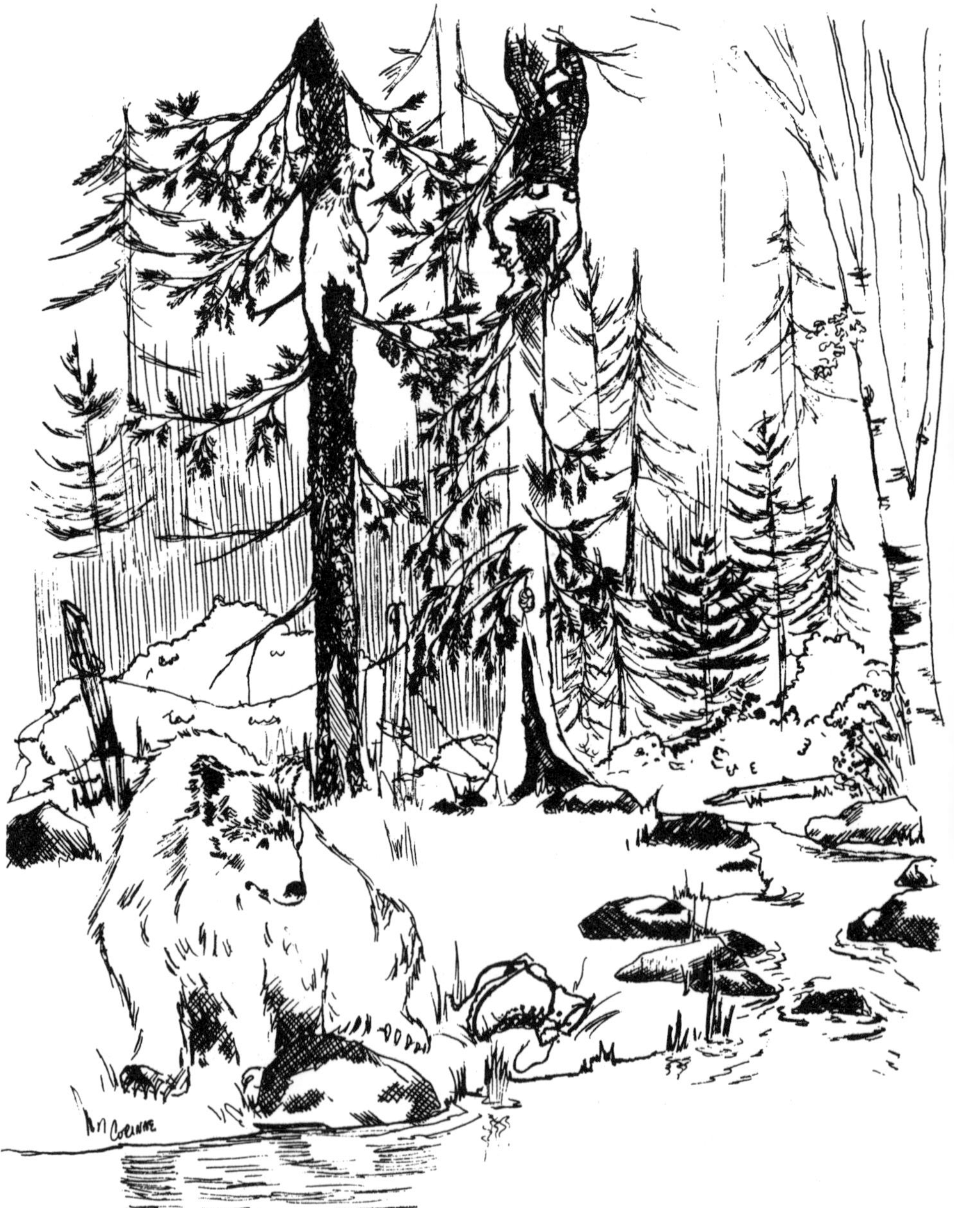
Corinne

minute or two I felt the tree shakin'. Good, I thought – she's goin' back the way she came. She just bumped into the hemlock.

Bumped into it alright – up she come. I had to use my escape route – the 3 limbs I had chosen. I held onto 2 of them and walked on the other back to the spruce. Of course once I got back to the spruce, she was up the hemlock. She started chewin' on the stubs where I had been standin'. She was some kinda ugly. I was watchin' her – no trouble to see.

Down the hemlock and up the spruce she came. Back into the hemlock I went. Once I made my first crossin' I started hollerin'. My neighbour Richard Feeney was always workin' on his machinery. The wind was comin' out of the southwest. The only chance I had was for him to hear me. I found out later that it was the only night of the week he wasn't outside. I crossed a dozen times in all.

Finally about an hour had gone by and my wife Judy come out. She heard me yellin'.

"I need help – get Richard."

It wasn't 5 minutes later I heard somebody say,

"George, where are ya?"

I recognized his voice. It was Richard Grasse.

I said, "Richard – get the heck out of here. A bear's got me up a tree and she'll kill you."

Around two minutes later Richard was back to my house in his car and on his way home.

About 5 minutes later I saw my car come off the road at Pat Feeney's place. It stopped at the first hill. Pat yelled,

"Where are ya?"

"I'm back here."

The next hill he come to he yelled,

"Where are ya?"

I said, "I'm back here. I'm up the bear tree."

He knew exactly where I was.

Pat and Judy drove in – they were back about 25 feet from the spruce tree. I was in the spruce at that time. When the car drove in, the bear moved back. Pat opened the door and I could look right inside the car, through the sun–roof. He didn't have a rifle with him. When he got out, I said,

"Where's your rifle?"

"What do I need a rifle for?"

I said, "A bear's got me up a tree."

"Oh my God," Pat said.

"Don't leave me," I yelled.

"No, no, we won't leave you."

Well, Richard Grasse landed there a few minutes later with a couple of rifles. When I saw the rifles I come down.

"She's not very far away, I can hear her," I said. "The only way to get the bear is to get the cub out of the tree."

So they shot the cub out of the tree and down she fell. It was whinin' layin' there so of course I finished it off. I ran back to the car and the mother was standin' there. Richard had a good shot at 'er but we never got her that night.

The next mornin' when I went to work – I was pretty shook up. The boss told me to take the day off.

That evening I was up that tree waitin'. The cub was layin' under the tree and I figured she'd come back. I only stayed until 6:30. There was lots of daylight. I was walkin' in when my wife and kids yelled,

"There's a bear on the hill."

I said, "What?"

They spelled it out, "BEAR". I exited into one of my other fields but I never found her. I expect it was the same bear. I never got that bear that year. On September 7, 1982 I shot a bear. I'd swear on a stack of Bibles it was the same bear. There's no way you could ever prove it.

Rippling Rivers

As told by Eva Searle

A holiday spent on Cains River and the Miramichi in 1917 may be interesting to those who fished there many years ago. As a teenager, in Ontario Mrs. Flora McCrea Eaton had longed to come to New Brunswick to take that fishing trip. She finally made it when she was married and had four sons.

In her diary she has told the fascinating story – she called it Rippling Rivers.

On July 20th (1917) she and her friend, Miss Annie Pringle, reached Cains River Bridge where Mr. Herb Freeze was waiting with canoes, guides and equipment. Then they were off on their adventure in the New Brunswick wilds.

Along Cains River they stayed at Duffies Camp and Hopewell Lodge. Of course, the ladies had to learn to cast for trout. Annie Pringle's guide was Dick, and part of Dick's instructions went something like this: "Oh, you jerked it too quick, miss. That's better – just draw it easy ... There's a rise. Now be CAREFUL. Oh – you were too quick. Try it again. Easy now – oh, he's off – you weren't quick enough. There's another rise. That's it. THAT'S IT!" – and Annie had her trout.

They fished Chestnut Pool and Gordon Brook, catching many 2 and 3 pounders. But they had to put up with a few discomforts. Insects swarmed and bit, heavy thunder storms seemed to pursue them. They had to climb up and down 90 steps between the beach and Hopewell Lodge. But there were no complaints – it was part of a fishing trip.

They left Cains River on the 3rd of August. At Blackville they were joined by other members of the family, and a few changes were made in the party. A new cook, tall and handsome, by the name of Arthur Green arrived. At Boiestown Herb Freeze had to leave and his place was taken by Mel Murphy. And there were two other guides, Donald and Henry.

Salmon fishing began in earnest on the Miramichi. The first day a 10 pounder and an 11 pounder were caught by a man of the party. Mrs. Eaton's reaction? – an incredulous "Why don't you shout? What's the use of catching anything if you keep so quiet about it?"

There were adventures at Half Moon Bridge, Camp Louis, McKeil Brook, Burnt Hill and Clearwater Camp.

August 22nd was their last day and Mrs. Eaton was up at 5:30 a.m. She became quite lyrical about washing her hair in the Miramichi at the break of dawn. She wrote: "Last dip and hair–wash in the soft and laughing waters of the Miramichi River. The water in the river is so soft one feels as if a smooth hand caressed and refreshed one." But promptly she returned to her forthright style: "At 5:30 a.m. a nice hot stove to place one's feet upon would add to the delight."

After breakfast they broke camp for the last time. They reached Boiestown in the early evening and boarded their train.

A quick and amusing tour through the Maritimes is recorded. On the way back to Ontario they stopped at Quebec City, and they met Col. Guthrie from Fredericton. When he heard about their guides of the Miramichi he said: "I know them all. In fact I have a son of Donald's and one of Henry's in my regiment."

In the foreword of the published diary, Mrs. Eaton said she had kept the diary for her own pleasure in the future. She generously added: "If it helps to pass an hour agreeably for someone, then it will have helped me again."

She wrote that diary in 1917. We read it, with pleasure, in 1995.

It is a beautifully bound book in soft brown leather, and in gold lettering: "Rippling Rivers. My Diary. Flora McCrea Eaton."

The book can be found in that treasure house of history – the New Brunswick Legislative Library.

Trout Fishing Years Ago

I am writing this story June 6, 1994 while reminiscing about the 'good old days' of fishing places like the Cains River, the Penniac Stream, the Miramichi River, Louis Lake, Peaked Mountain Lake.

I'll never forget the first time my Uncle Bill took my father, Ron and me twenty–five miles to a pristine wilderness area. It was June 1965 – no clear– cutting – no pollution – few vehicles – lots of game and twenty–five miles through rugged terrain back of Doaktown. Valentine and Island Lakes were to become one of my favourite places to angle for years to come. On that first trip we fiorded the Dungarvon River and trekked the last five miles by foot. We unpacked, took our fishing gear and headed down a woods trail to the shore where we spotted the wooden raft we were going to use. I stepped in what appeared to be four inches of water and sank out of sight in the muck bottom. Dad reached down a pole, I grabbed it and he pulled me out.

"You have to watch your step around here son – that bottom is just like quick–sand."

"Thanks for the warning – I found out the hard way."

There were a few other facts that I learned very quickly about these lakes: there were a lot of Papa and Mama speckles for the taking and there were lots of leeches 5–6 inches long!

The trout that we caught in the early years were the true native fish. They had a royal navy blue tinge, magnificent coloured speckles and their insides were beet red in colour. They were the best trout I've ever eaten and many other fishermen such as Richard Kitchen, Ralph Hatto, Randy Campbell, Vernon Mooers, Fred Morton, Ken Flemming, and Terry Goguen have echoed similar comments. The trout were also terrific scrappers. The average size in the early years was 13–14 inches whereas today a 10 incher is hard to find. All of the trout today are stocked and the lakes are fished to death. There are more new roads going in and around the lake than Carter has pills. Clear–cutting is rampant with former stands of beautiful wilderness being reduced to barren rubble. This of course is being done in the name of commerce. What a joke! Maybe I'm just a purist at heart but I shudder to think what the future holds for New Brunswickers and their forests.

I have fished these lakes so many times with successful results that a friend of mine Bill Page said, "Peter, you have cracked the code."

I'd like to tell you about one of those trips which began on a frosty morning in early May 1978. My brother Ron and I slid the 16 foot Chestnut Ogilvie canoe into the back of my heaterless Volkswagon camper and took off. The tailgate was wide open so you can appreciate the fact that it was rather chilly.

Ron and I are alike in many ways and enjoy each other's company. The two hour journey passes quickly when we are together discussing topics like fishing, hunting and hockey. That particular morning we sighted 7 white– tailed deer, 3 partridge and a couple of rabbits alongside the road. I told Ron the story of the great luck three fishermen from Saint John that Dave Cochrane and I watched land 25 huge trout last year. Their catch averaged about 2 pounds and two weighed in at 3 1/2 pounds They caught them on Island Lake using live minnows. We were two excited fishermen – that's for sure.

For anyone new to lake fishing for trout – the best time of the year for fishing is during the ice break up and immediately after the ice goes out. The fish are ravenous.

When we arrived, we noticed that two other trucks were already there. We set our minnow traps baited with bread in the culvert and we sat in the camper sipping piping hot coffee from Ron's new thermos.

The sky was cloudy – the temperature had risen considerably and there was scarcely a wrinkle on the water. This was a crucial factor. There were just slight puffs of wind – first from the east and then from the north. It was just what the doctor ordered.

We launched my 16 foot Chestnut Ogilvie canoe and once on the lake, it didn't take us long to snap into action. We began spot fishing using night-crawlers. Ron was using a 9 foot Daiwa graphite rod with a Hardy Viscount salmon reel. I had an 8 1/2 foot Fenwick glass rod with a similar reel. After about an hour of fruitless labour – we headed for shore.

Back in the camper we sipped coffee, then grabbed our newly trapped batch of minnows, headed back out on the lake, and were soon back in business. Our comrades hadn't budged from their spots near the opposite shore. We decided to paddle around while looking for a series of newly formed lily pads or a wake of a fish. Ron spotted a roll of a trout. In a matter of seconds we were carefully anchored in close proximity to Ron's sighting. Ron attached the fly hook behind the dorsal fin of a minnow and cast out.

His minnow scarcely lighted on the water when the surface erupted. A lunker seized the defenceless minnow in a cannibalistic charge. Ron's rod became double-bent and he snapped the rod back – nothing except his bare hook. I told him not to worry.

"Never send a boy to do a man's job", I joked.

I put on the largest minnow in the bucket and popped it towards the identical spot. "Jaws" erupted the surface in a vicious attack and torpedoed towards the bottom, stripping my cortland line. I set the hook and the barb held firmly in place. The fish swam right towards the reeds but I held him tight. The leader cut across the surface like a straight razor cutting through paper as the fish spun off in different directions. After a good 4–5 minute battle, Mr. Forktail was dip netted by Ron. It was a real corker around 17" and a solid 2 1/2 pounder.

Now it was Ron's turn to cast towards the cluster of green foliage. In a matter of seconds – another strike. He pointed the tip of his rod skywards ever so gently waiting until he was certain that his trout was hooked securely. He tightened up slowly and the hook held. The fish stripped off his line like a salmon.

"That one is a monster. It's the Moby Dick of Island Lake. It feels like a 5 pounder", he screamed.

The water spewed in all directions as the gigantic trout did a back-flip on the top of the water. Ron's reel clinked and clanked as the trout fought desperately for its life. Finally the battle was over and I

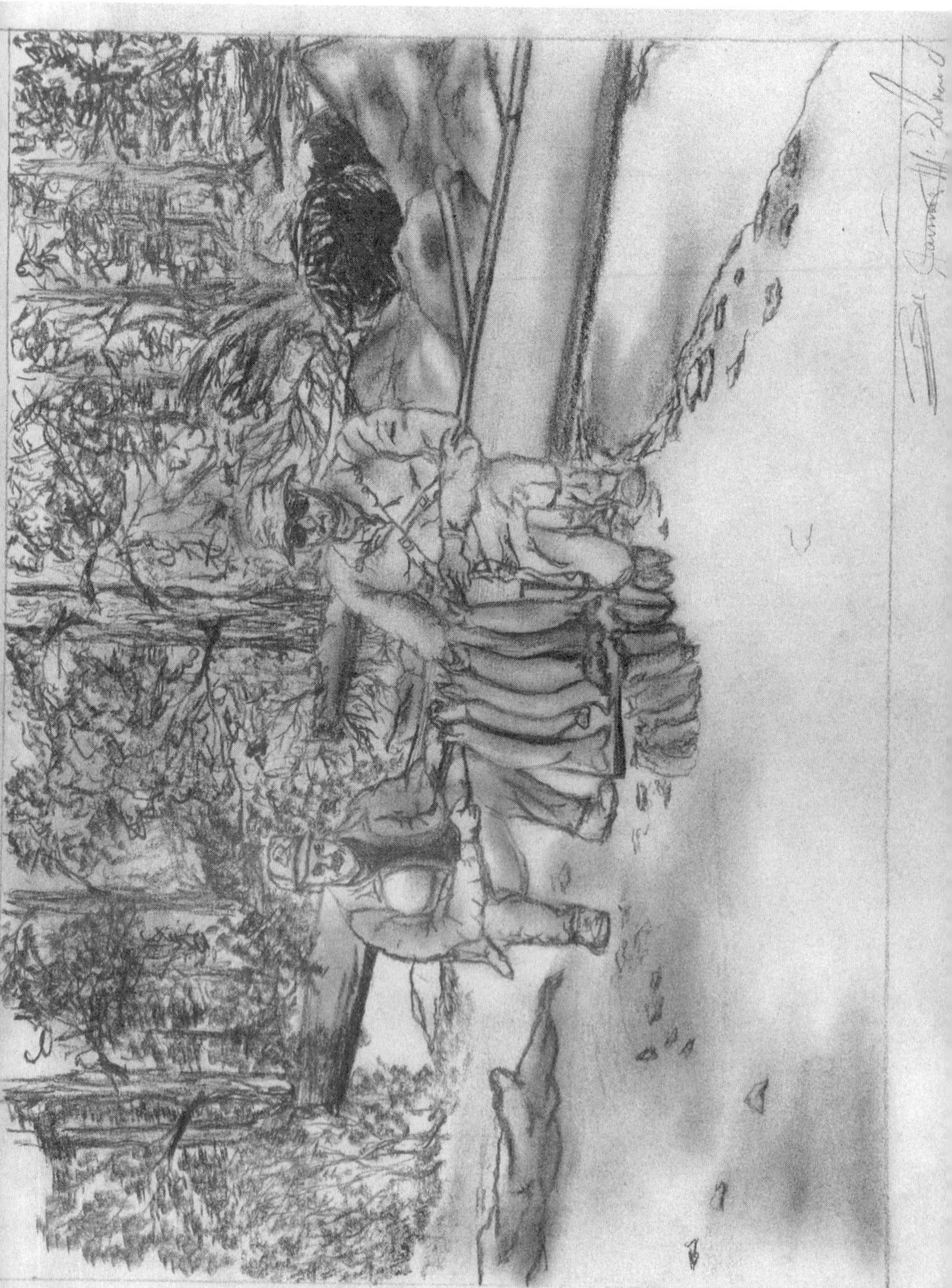

netted the beauty. I laid it in the cooler beside the other – twins.

Within an hour we had amassed a really nice catch. We didn't have our limits of 15 each but we didn't care. The solitary boat remaining made a bee– line straight towards us after they realized we were catching a few. They wanted to know what we were using as they anchored alongside us.

"Flies and night crawlers are as good as anything" I told them. Neither Ron nor I was about to reveal the truth.

Ron attached a juicy night crawler and I tied on a number six Royal Wulff dry fly. I nailed a 1 1/2 pound trout and Ron did likewise. Then a huge fish rolled up and snatched a may–fly off the surface. I cast the dry fly to the exact location and up from the depths came a humungous trophy. He jumped completely out of the water and pounced upon my fly as a cat would snatch at a bird. I tightened up – too late – I was out of luck. This rascal had sampled the menu and spat it out hastily.

The other three gentlemen cast their wares in the approximate area with no success. We stayed in the same general location as did our neighbours for another hour. The school of fish vanished, which is often the case in lake fishing – feast or famine.

We had a total of 23 trout with an average of 1 1/2 pounds. We left for home two happy fishermen. The good old days – when you told about the "whoppers" you caught – and it was the truth!

My First Teaching Position

as told by Murray Sargeant

[Murray Sargeant was superintendent in school districts 26 and 27 (Fredericton, McAdam and Harvey) from 1955-1971.]

There's quite a story that happened in 1923. Jobs were very very scarce at that time in teaching and I made a number of applications. I got an answer from nobody. My cousin, Bill Sargeant went to Normal School. I didn't want to be a sponge on my parents so I got a job at the Sugar Refinery for the summer. Then one day about five days before school was about to open, my cousin Bill came up to the house. He said,

"Murray, I got two acceptances today – one for Black River and one for Smithtown. I'm going to take the Black River job, why don't you take the Smithtown job.

I said, "I can't do that, my name's not Bill Sargeant."

He said, "Don't tell them. Don't tell them at all. I don't know where the place is – but you may find it."

Well, anyway my father had an old Ford car and Bill and I drove to Smithtown which was just outside Hampton. On the way into Smithtown my cousin ran over some hens and he killed one of them.

I said to my cousin, "That settles my job."

When I got to the interview they didn't ask me a question. It was a poor district. It had gotten a good grant from the government. I had a special license called a "superior license" because I had first year college education. They were delighted when they heard that. They offered me a job.

I said, "I'm not Bill Sargeant, I'm Murray Sargeant."

I could have been the worst teacher in the world and I could have been pretty good. The teacher before me had needed only half a year's teaching to collect his retirement pension. He had been living on the parish – in the poorhouse. The board thought it only fair to get him off the parish so they gave him a term contract.

The first day of school I introduced myself. I was 17 1/2 at the time. There were 43 students from grades 1–10 in a one–room schoolhouse. After grade ten, students could attend Normal School. Shortly after I got started, that first day, I heard a sort of rumble coming down the road. I looked out to see what it was. There was a sloven – a sort of wagon low to the ground being driven by one of the neighbours. Next thing you know – the doors opened – the windows went up and everybody clammered outside. They apparently went out to chat with this fellow.

I went out and was just gawking. I questioned a student,

"What gives – what's going on here?"

I was informed that anytime a sloven, car or anything else passed the students would rush to see who was there. I put a damper on that business right smartly.

Then shortly after that – the roof leaked. I went to the secretary of the school and expressed my concerns about the youngsters.

She said "We can't do anything about it."

I said "What about the youngsters?"

She said "Have a bi–social."

I said "I don't know what good a bi–social will be in fixing my roof. Furthermore, I don't even know what a bi–social is."

As it turned out, the bi–social was a fund–raising event that got us enough money to fix the roof. I had a great time at that school. I was there only one year.

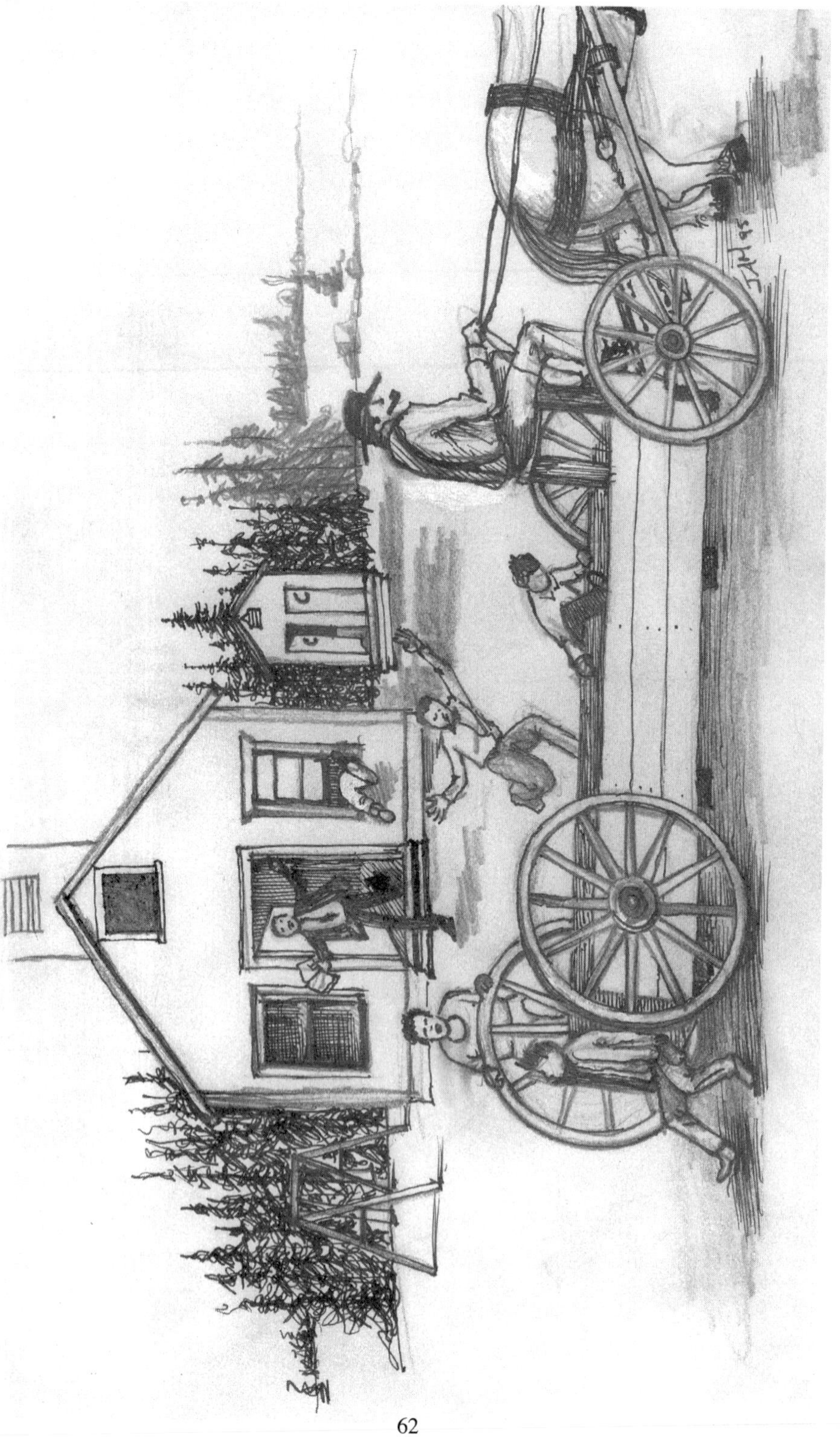

Reddy Fox 1913-1973

Grant Fox was a lifelong resident of Fredericton. Many of us have heard the expression, "Some people are a product of their environment." Such was the case with Grant. Perley and Maud were the names of Grant's father and mother and he had a sister Blanche.

Grant went as far as grade four in school. He was very belligerent and unruly – whether he was expelled or left on his own is uncertain.

Perley was an excellent stone–cutter by trade and sold tombstones first at King Street and then from his residence at 509 Aberdeen Street.

Grant went to work for his father at an early age as an apprentice. Perley knew how to move the heavy tombstones with relative ease. Grant acquired the special skills of cutting, imprinting letters, quoting prices and transporting the monuments and learned the business from top to bottom.

A neighbour, Tilley Daley, recollects an event told by Grant's cousin. One day while walking down town Grant saw a boy his age eating an ice cream cone. Grant begged his father to buy him one but his pleas fell on deaf ears. Grant's father was very cruel. He scarcely gave him a nickel for working, never called him by name and bossed him around like a slave. Grant never forgave him for his cruel treatment. On the other hand, his mother was well liked and respected by Grant. Maud was insanely jealous of her husband Perley. Wherever he went – she went. She kept a close eye on him day and night.

Grant joined the army in the Second World War. He was in the artillery unit and later honorably dismissed because of a broken eardrum. Upon returning home he again worked with the family business and lived with his parents on Argyle Street, Fredericton. Those who remember Grant in the early years say that he was clean-cut in appearance, friendly to talk to and a fine looking man to boot.

When Grant's mother took sick several years before she died, Grant waited on her hand and foot. His father was bedridden before he died as well. My neighbour Ernie Scott related the fact that his brother Bill Scott went to check up on Perley. When he left the premises he told Grant that his father needed to see a doctor. Grant issued a warning saying that no doctor was coming inside his house. Bill went and brought the doctor anyway. Maud died on August 29, 1960 and Perley died the following day, August 30, of a heart attack.

After his mother and father died Grant changed his lifestyle completely. He wouldn't allow his sister, who was then Mrs. Blanche Flemming, into his house. A neighbour, Mrs Myrtle Ferris, remembers Grant breaking the family dishes and burying them in a hole in the backyard. He also refused to give one red cent of the inheritance to his sister.

Thus began the life of Reddy the Fox as we came to know him. The kids at St. Dunstan's School were terrified of him. He had a fence in his backyard and if a soccer ball, tennis ball or anything else landed there – no one would climb the fence to retrieve their personal belongings. Reddy stopped shaving and getting haircuts. Pat Delong called him "Fredericton's First Real Hippie". In the early 60's this husky man with the long matted ponytail and black rubber boots walked or biked the streets of Fredericton. He became known as a collector of bottles, in particular. He felt that there was going to be a bottle shortage some day. He also picked up pieces of wood, iron and just about anything else you could think of.

People in the neighbourhood felt sorry for him. If someone wanted to help him out he would likely say that he needed no help or that he was just fine. Neighbours remembered the fact that Reddy ate a lot

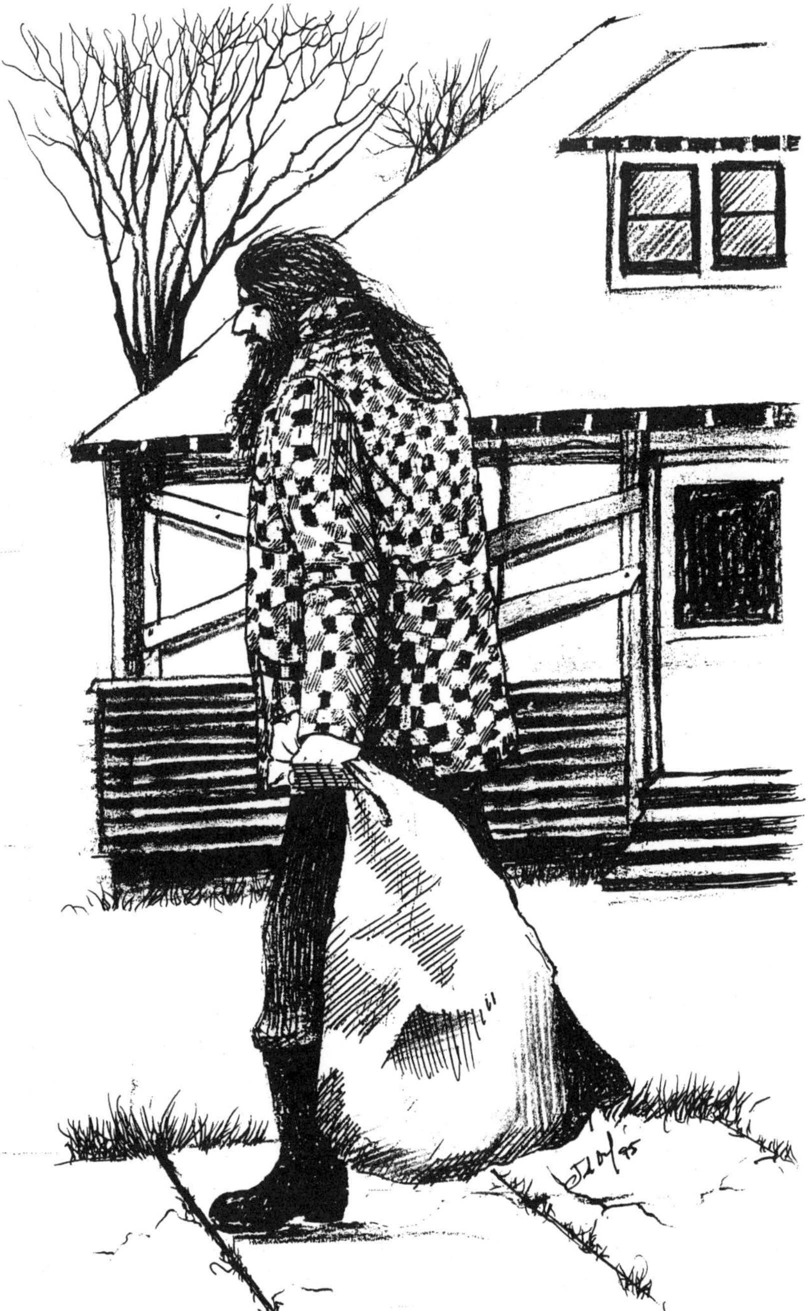

of apples but that he hated to part with a dime. He was often seen buying wood at the Farmers' Market Saturday mornings. Reddy lived in the kitchen of the house and closed the rest of the house off. He refused to pay the power and water bills so he was cut off. Imagine living for years in Fredericton with no running water or electricity.

Pat Delong remembers an act of kindness from Reddy. It seems that one summer Reddy found an unattended ball glove at Queen Square. He knew Les Delong and he brought it to the door.

"Les, I believe one of your sons left this glove at the ballfield."

The majority of the people I talked to confirm that Reddy was an odd character but relatively harmless. Kids tormented and teased him something awful. They broke almost every window out of his house. He bought some plywood and boarded up all of the windows.

Alfred Burgoyne, a teacher and later the principal at St. Dunstan's School, recalled an incident where some kids from Oromocto were playing soccer against St. Dunstan's School. One of the kids threw a rock at Reddy's house. The next day, Reddy came storming into Alfred's class clasping a good-sized rock.

He shouted,

"Either these kids stop throwing rocks at my house or someone's going to get a boulder in the head." Alfred said he had to take him out in the hallway to calm him down. On another occasion, one of the travelling art teachers took the kids outside to sketch houses. A couple of the students decided to draw Reddy's. He wasn't long in putting the run to them. He had no idea what the kids were doing or why they would want to draw his house.

In 1968 Reddy dislocated his shoulder and arrived at the Victoria Public Hospital without a medicare card. He held out a wad of bills and said "will this do" and was promptly admitted. They cut his hair and cleaned him up. You can imagine the mess. Some say that he insisted on having his matted hair saved and when he left the hospital somehow managed to re-attach his original hair.

Tilley Daley remembered the fact that two weeks before Grant died, he visited Fox's barber shop where he had his beard shaved and hair cut. She also remembers him getting his best suit drycleaned about the same time.

He died in March 1973 from cancer. His sister Blanche A.D.

Flemming at Lakeville inherited the property valued at eight thousand dollars as well as a personal estate of approximately $34,831.87. There was a mint condition truck in the shed as well. His veranda was chockful of various bottles. Reddy is still remembered by many as a "man of mystery" because few people ever really knew him. One must adhere to the expression "Never criticize until you have walked a mile in one's shoes."

Sam Satter

Sam Satter along with his horse and wagon were a familiar sight in the Fredericton streets for over four decades. His particular business was buying and selling scrap metals, rags and bottles.

Sam was born in Warsaw, Poland in 1900. His family included 3 sisters and 5 brothers. All of his sisters died of scarlet fever at an early age. Sam worked in the family bakery business. Around 1920 he immigrated to Canada on a refugee boat along with Rose, his wife to be. Sam worked at a butcher's shop and at a bakery for a few years in Fredericton. Rose worked at the Hartt Shoe Company.

It is rumoured that when Sam and Rose opened up the scrap and bottle business at 260 King Street in the early 1930s he paid the fee of $15,000 in $1000 bills. Sam and Rose worked very hard and were well known in the community. Sam would take his horse and wagon to the streets and Rose would look after affairs in the yard at home.

Don Daley remembers helping Sam on his rounds on Saturday mornings in the 30's with another friend. One of the boys would guard the wagon and the other would help Sam load the bottles and rags and burlap bags onto the wagon. At the day's end Sam would reward each boy with a 10-cent piece. Don remembers Sam as being "a great guy."

Vella Mooers Schwartz remembers Sam stopping on her street in the 40's and bellowing at the top of his lungs, "Any rags, any bags, any bottles today?"

During the Second World War Sam's family and many relatives were murdered by the Nazis at Auschwitz. Sam never returned to his

Computer Drawing by Alex McGibbon

native homeland.

Ed Gorman, a former city police officer, who walked the beat for 22 years remembers the Satters.

"I remember Sam and Rose quite well. Sam was a bit shy until he got to know you. Rose was very outgoing. I'd walk by and Rose would invite me in for a coffee and a cookie or donut. She was very warm-hearted. I remember the Satter household as being spic and span – the house was immaculate. A lot of people never knew that Sam and Rose were very generous. Sam would often buy the "down and out" coffees and breakfasts. Sam often gave a quarter to those children he felt could use it. Rose collected clothes from the Jewish community and come winter she'd clothe many of the poor of the community. I used to call her 'an angel in disguise'. That couple were some of the kindest people I've ever met."

Sam may not have had much formal education but he was what you'd call street smart. He could talk on just about any subject in Russian, Polish, German, or English. Sam read any newspaper he could get his hands on. One of Sam's favorite past-times was to go to either the Gaiety or Capital Theatre. Dick Howland remembers seeing Sam at the Capital in the same end – aisle row seat on a regular basis.

Sam knew his customers by first and last name and would often spend time sharing the latest news.

I remember in the early 60's seeing Sam coming up Chestnut Street. You could hear the plop, plop, plop of his horse's shoes hitting the pavement. He had a big grey beard and a booming voice. The other kids and myself stared in awe and trepidation as we watched this character. I remember one time my younger brother Jim stole some bottles – ran over to the next street and sold them back. I'm sure he wasn't the only kid to pull a prank like that. The irony of my brother stealing a few bottles is that he later dated Natalie Satter – Sam's granddaughter. He also worked with Sam's son Sidney.

Sam never worried much about what people thought about him holding up the 5 o'clock traffic downtown or on the old Carleton Street Bridge. They might yell obscenities – honk their horns or physically threaten him. He didn't care so long as he took care of his business. He might yell something like

"I've got a business to run – I've got a business to run." Eventually the city forced Sam to take his horse and wagon off the streets in the early 70's. He never officially retired although his son Sidney took over the business. In September of 1982 Sam died when fire and smoke engulfed his house on King Street.

Sidney was also a good will ambassador in the community. He sponsored many teams over the years. He was also involved in the sport of bowling. He was very fair with his workers and most often gave them drives to and from work.

Whenever I and many other Fredericton residents cashed in bottles with Sid he'd always say for a dollar "Here's a hundred dollar bill" and smile. He was a great guy and well–respected. Sid passed away in June 1994 of cancer. His wife Freda told me that during Sid Satter's funeral procession that there was a police officer on every corner. Each and everyone saluted as a signal of honour and a tribute to a remarkable man.

Both Sam and Sidney Satter will always be remembered by many for their contributions to the community.

Fact & Fancy

CFNB Radio

Jack Fenety wanted to become a forester as he had a great affinity for the outdoors. However, due to a war-time accident he was unable to pursue this goal. Upon arriving home after the Second World War he met up with an old friend, Malcolm Neill, who informed Jack that he was taking over the C.F.N.B. radio station. His father was retiring.

In October 1945 Malcolm gave Jack a job announcing that lasted over four decades up to January 1988. These were some of the best years of his life and Jack states that he loved his job so much that he probably would have worked for no pay.

When Jack broke into the broadcasting business he began as a trainee radio announcer. Later on that year Jack began announcing the local midnight news. In those days it was a joke among the listeners that Jack was funnier than the likes of Jack Benny, Red Skelton or Bob Hope. He was so nervous and made so many mistakes – you wouldn't believe it. In those days, as far back as the commencement of the station in 1923, Frederictonians didn't go to bed until after the midnight news. They wanted to know where the firetruck went or why the police department was seen at a residence on King Street. They stayed up with their sardines, crackers and a cup of tea, their ears glued to the magic box. A school teacher would call and say, "Jack I heard you say so and so. I taught you better than that. You know that's not the way I taught you in school."

On and on it went. There is nothing tougher than working in your hometown. People are hard on you. Jack says, "I came, I saw, I conquered." It was a long hard grind — with lots of laughs and a few tears.

Jack's tremendous God-given abilities didn't go unnoticed. His voice had a distinct timbre, well-suited to radio and in 1947 he was given the opportunity to have his own special program. His "Fact and Fancy" show ran for a total of over 13,000 programs and was heard by tens of thousands of listeners. His audience included people from Maine to Newfoundland. Jack referred to his program as "the generation program" geared specifically for women: daughters, mothers, grandmothers and great-great grandmothers. There were poems read by Jack submitted by some of New Brunswick's budding poets. There were household hints and recipes and notices of meetings interspersed with music for the listener.

Once Jack took a couple of days off to go fishing. His replacement was Bud Brown Jr. Bud was giving out a recipe on how to make coffee cake. When he finished he stated,

"I see that whoever sent this recipe in forgot to give the amount of coffee needed. I'll play a record and see if I can come up with the proper quantity of coffee."

The switchboard became jammed with calls. Needless to say Bud was the laughing stock of the station for quite some time.

Jack had many a man that would write, call or stop him in the street and say,

"What do you mean? Good morning ladies – I'm not a lady and I listen to your program – so does my cousin Fred." Jack would reply with his standard answer. "I want to tell you what I tell all of the other gentlemen friends. This program was designed for the ladies but I have no objection if the men want to tune in."

From time to time Jack used to wrangle with Bob Dickeson, the local meteorologist. It seems that on different occasions Jack and Bob wouldn't see eye to eye. Jack claims that a certain portion of his audience would listen to him even though he had no meteorological training, only "natural observation training".

Jack was and still is remembered as an outspoken conservationist and in 1961 he was made president for life of the Miramichi Salmon Association.

All of us who remember Jack wish him the best. We will always remember his "Fact and Fancy" show.

Charlie Clayton's Camps

I've lived out here in the Penniac area since I was 8 years old. My family moved here from Marysville in 1910. I've worked in the woods logging and guiding all my life.

At one time I had a cook camp and two sleepin' camps for sports at Penniac. I also had four camps, 5 miles out here at the head of East Brook. I had awful good luck gettin' sports. Prior to the Second World War I just had a few parties. I was in the war for four years. After the war, I started guidin' again and I could get sports left and right every year for twenty years.

I treated everybody fair and square. I never paid any attention to what walk of life my sports were from – as long as they paid me. We generally got pretty good tips. The huntin' back then was real good. We hunted bear in the spring – deer, woodcock and partridge in the fall.

Sometimes the sports would end up with their limits – sometimes they would go back with nuthun'. Sometimes they would come here with clothes that wasn't fit to be used – clothes that they used for duck huntin' – clothes that you could hear them two miles away. Others came and had extra good luck right off the bat. I found that it depended on the travellin' of the deer. When the bucks were travellin' they'd get no deer. I remember back in November we'd get no doe – only buck. A lot of the sports didn't care what they shot.

One party came here ten years in a row. They didn't care if they ever shot a deer. They wanted to get away from their offices – away from city life – away from the telephone. They just wanted to get in the woods and enjoy themselves.

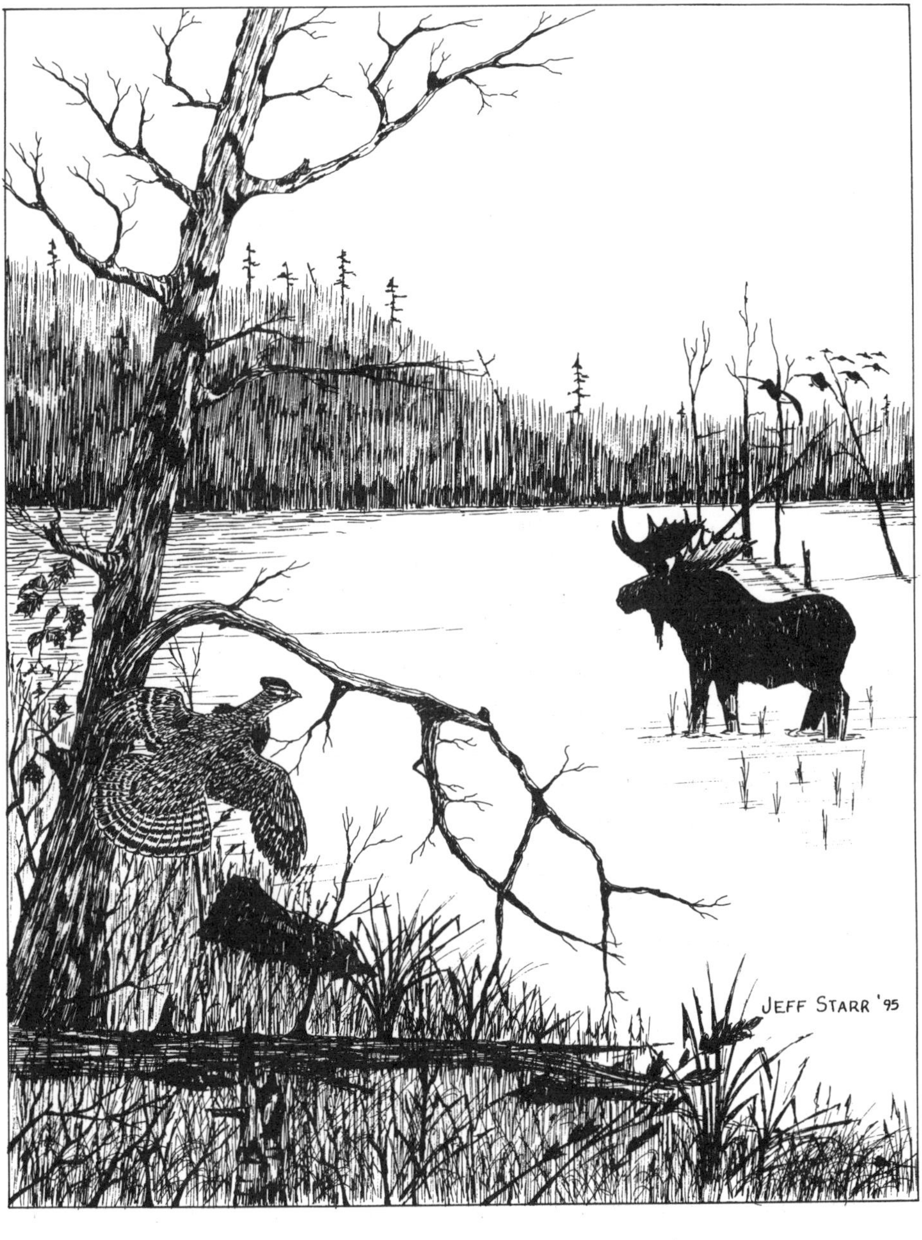
JEFF STARR '95

Guidin' was fun back then – hard times or not – I was younger and pretty tough. The sports were all a bunch of good fellahs.

Many of the sports wouldn't drink any alcohol – others did nothing but drink. I'd lay the law down. When they got here on Sunday I'd let them know that if they were drinkin' in the mornin' – we don't go out. Drink all you want at night but if anyone is drinking in the morning – you'll be staying in the camp.

I hired the best guides I could find – guys who were reliable – guys that knew the woods. In l961 the guides made $36.00 – $45.00 for a week's work. Some of the guides that worked for me: James Gilmore (Moose), Arthur Allen, Bob Allen, Raymond Chase, Ernie Chase, Lawrence Mann, Ted Gibson and Bill Whitty. When the sports went home happy – the guides made good tips.

I hired first–class cooks – the best money could buy. Some of the cooks that worked for me were: Allen Saunders, Norman Scott, Boyd Cleveland and Raymond McGivney. We used to take in quite a load of grub. I can remember spendin' 500 dollars for a week's grub. There was everything you can imagine. We fed our sports as good as they'd get in any high class restaurant. For breakfast they got homefries, choice of bacon or ham with eggs, home–made toast, juices, coffee or tea – the works. Sometimes we'd come back for lunch – not very often. Generally we'd take a raw piece of roast beef or deer with us – some sandwiches – some cake. We'd cook that piece of meat on a stick over a small fire – put a little salt to it – mister man there ain't much better. It'd taste better than you could get at the camp or anywhere else.

For supper – now that was a big meal. We'd have beef or turkey, chicken or pork. It'd change everyday. There would be fresh rolls, taters, fresh vegetables, home–made bread, pies, cakes plus all the trimmings. They ate like kings – all they could eat.

I was quite a practical joker at times. One time I got stung. On one occasion I boasted to Mr. and Mrs. Pittkin that a bear's liver was a delicacy. Well, Mr. Pittkin shot a bear and the cook, Allen Saunders, served the liver for supper. Of course they made sure I had a rather generous portion. This was one time where the joke backfired and of course I had to bear the brunt of my own misfortune. I'll never forget swallowing each mouthful of that liver. It was terrible.

Charlie kept in contact with many of his former sports for many years. The following are some of the excerpts from letters Charlie received of how the sports felt about coming to Charlie's Camps in Penniac, New Brunswick and hunting:

Dear Charlie:

Boy! Oh! Boy! that 14 pointer weighed 214 lbs dressed on the hoof. Believe me if I live to be a hundred I'll never forget that 14 pointer. If you ever hear me say there aren't big deer in your camps – please crown me with a log.

P.S. The deer weighed about 275 lbs. when I shot it. By next November that

14 pointer should weigh at least 350 lbs.

Yours very truly,

George Schiefer
Syracuse, N.Y.

Hans Zillessen, a renowned artist from New York, wrote:

Dear Charlie:

It was tough at first getting back to all that noise and commotion of the New York City rush. Sometimes I realize that I am really not "cut out" for this sort of living. Needless to say the week hunting with you was a great tonic. I would have liked to stay another week, as I was just beginning to hit my old stride and vigor.

Always Your Partner

Hans

Dear Charlie: (Christmas)

You should see the little balsam fir now, all a–glitter, and reminding me so often of Penniac, East Brook and all the silent miles you and I have travelled together – the laughs, the good hot coffee over a nice fire. I see the friendly Canada Jay paying us a visit to see what we are having for lunch, and suddenly I can see the big buck travelling like a ghost through all that brush and a second later I see us walking up to him – it was very wonderful and let's hope we can repeat it in the New Year.

Dear Charlie:

I won't go anywhere this fall. I had a stroke about the 26th of August. Oh how I wish to sneak off and hunt with Charlie Clayton a little bit and laugh with him. I surely spent some of my happiest moments of my life with you in those woods. Hope sincerely that I'll be getting up there again. Have a grand hunting season! I am going to be with you in my thoughts and laugh with you too.

                         Always Your Partner
                         Hans
                         Long Beach, New York

Ted Farnsworth wrote more than once:

Dear Charlie,

All in all we had a good hunt and a very good time up there. You and your guides were very good to us and we liked everything very much. The food was wonderful and plenty of it. The camps were very good and we were very comfortable at all times. The guide service was wonderful at all times. I sure would have liked to stay for 2 or 3 more days. I'm sure I would have gotten some deer.

Dear Charlie:

Hey Charlie that cook Ray McGivney, we thought was tops with us. He sure is a fine cook in my book so you don't have to change by our book. Believe me we all know good cooking. Those cakes, pies and cookies were the best and the rest of the food was first class also. We may have kidded him a bit but it was all in fun. When we are out on a vacation and hunting or fishing we sure like to have a good time.

                    Yours truly,
                    Ted Farnsworth
                    Pittsburgh, Mass.

Another gentleman, Dr. Simeon L. Carson sent Charlie a Christmas gift over the period of many years – a 20 dollar bill. He writes:

I am enclosing a small bill with which I wish you would buy something for the kiddies. Kindest regards to all. Hoping to see you later.

                    Very truly yours,

                    S.L. Carson
                    Washington, D.C.

I'm 85 years old and I'm tellin' you about the best years of my life.

What I'd give to be young again, if I could go back in time.

The Nondescript Davey, called the Man Bear

Where he came from and what he is. Inevitable facts which tell of Man's Inhumanity and its Results

THE DISCOVERY

The Daily Liberal, published at Halifax, contained the following item of news.

"A strange creature was noticed by a party of lumbermen upon the banks of the Salmon River. They claim that it is part bear and part human. The face bore a distinct resemblance to the human species. As they approached it they heard it groan and growl like a bear. As soon as the nondescript saw the party it ran from them rapidly, walking upon all fours."

In the summer of 1880, the St. John's Conservative told the following story:

"THE HUMAN BEAR"

Seen again on the Salmon River

"There never was so congenial a party of fishermen as the company of artists and actors that for the past two weeks have been camping

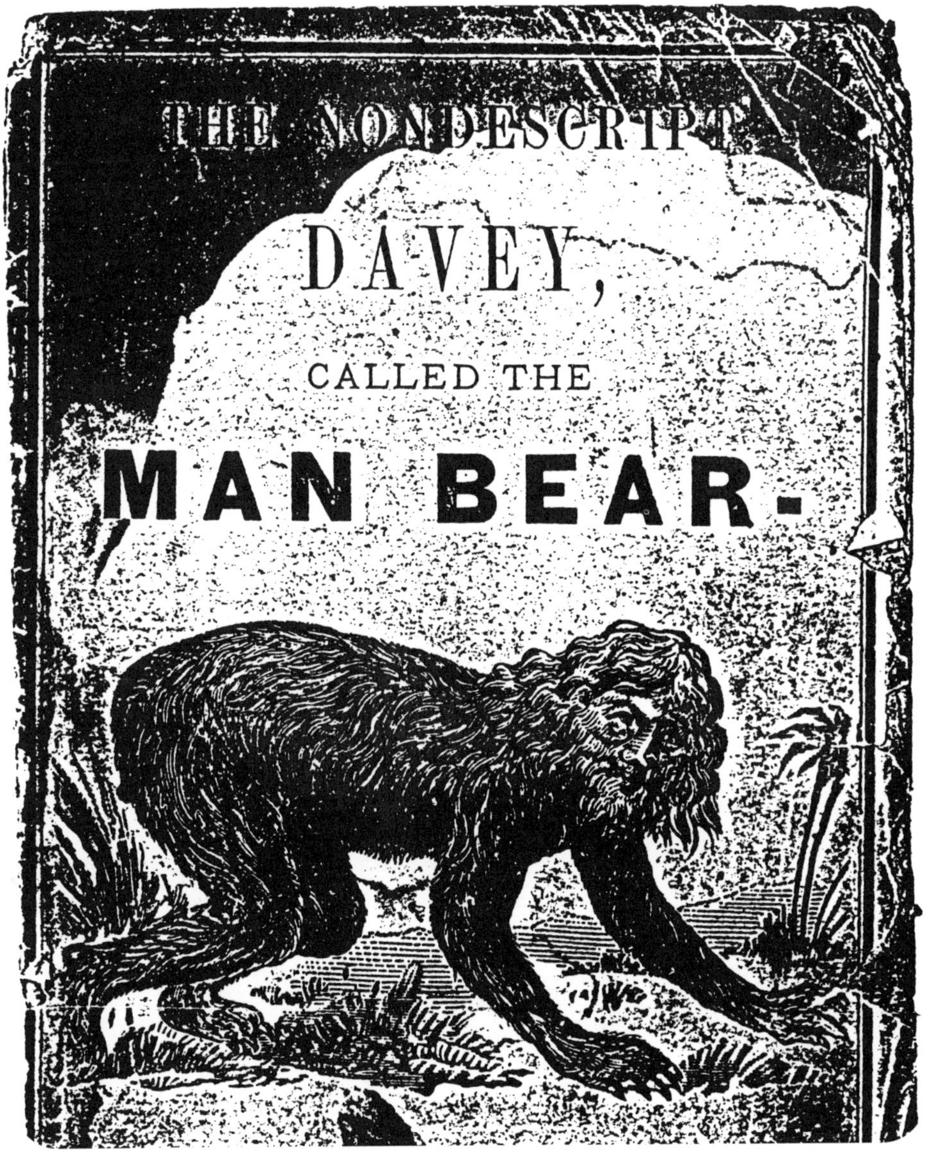
THE NONDESCRIPT.
DAVEY,
CALLED THE
MAN BEAR.

along the Salmon River. By mutual consent the actors have been supplying the artists with food, in return for which the artists were to decorate the rooms of the Outlandish Club in New York City with sketches of their tour. Harry Thomas, John Durking, and Charley Graham are artists who always seek pleasure, no matter at what cost; Frank Bush, John Whiston and Alt Burnett are a trio of humorists that even the solitude of the forest cannot dampen; Ralph Bayard, James Snedden and Harry Palmer form a press triplet, who are continually playing pranks. Under these circumstances, the public can naturally infer that the camp of the Outlandish Club did not resemble a cemetery.

"For a day or two one of the party was selected by lot to remain in camp as guard over the valuables of the party, which consisted mostly of wicker baskets, marked "glass with care."

"As no one ever came near, they finally considered a guard useless, and the camp was left to guard itself. The first day the party found all intact upon their return. The second day there was a cry of dismay. Whiston discovered that some one had broken into his hat box, and that the beaver, which he valued because it had been left to him by his father, was gone. The baskets marked "glass with care" had been broken open, and bottles lay strewn upon the ground.

One after the other was accused of the act of vandalism. When it was discovered that the bottles had not been opened, the Club, in Committee of the Whole, exonerated each other.

Day after day passed, and little articles of clothing were missed. Finally open boxes of canned fruit disappeared. A volunteer was called for to watch day before yesterday, and Whiston cheerfully stepped to the front.

Early in the morning they left him to his solitary vigil. He dressed himself with care. The blue shirt gave place to a white one, the hunting suit was replaced by his best broadcloth and Uncle John commenced to revive the memories of his facial business by giving a matinee to the forest trees. Tired with his exertions he laid down upon his bed of green boughs. At night when the Club returned to camp a sorry sight met their eye. Mingled among a dozen empty bottles lay the inanimate form of Whiston, his clothes were rags, his hair matted with blood, and face and arms were torn as if by sharp claws. In spite of his well known temperance proclivities his comrades feared that he had been enjoying the wine. After some trouble he was resuscitated and told the following story:

"I had lain down with no idea of going to sleep. I must have dropped off. On awakening I saw the most extraordinary brute. Moving upon all fours, like a bear, it was coolly knocking off the heads of the wine bottles and pouring the good stuff into its ugly carcass. Its face and body was covered with dirt and filth, and upon its misshapen head was my hat.

"At first it acted as if it was afraid. That encouraged me and I concluded to recover my property. I made a grab for the hat and it got me. Then there was a struggle. I have faint recollections of the brute trying to pour wine down my throat, and that is all."

"The boys are still trying to believe John's story."

It was on the nineteenth of June, 1881, that Daniel Mott and H.E. Sproul met the strange creature. Mott, in his excitement, fired at the human animal. Astonished and frightened, it turned and ran from him on all fours. Sproul and Mott gave chase. After a run of a mile and a half they saw the creature crawling into a hole in the rocky hillside. They determined to follow and capture it alive. Securing pine knots and dry bushes they kindled a fire near the entrance. The wind drove the smoke into the cave. It was more than the brute could stand, and he was forced to come forth. A short struggle with the half suffocated creature was enough to make him submissive, yet as a matter of safety he was securely bound.

An examination shows the following peculiar

ANATOMICAL FORMATION

The head thickly covered with long matted hair, black as jet. A line or ridge divided the occipital portion of the skull into two parts, the animal largely predominating over the intellectual. The ears were small and hearing quick. The jaw–bones protrude and possess a double action. No molars are in the mouth, and the teeth were evidently perfect at birth. The lips and mouth turn up in the same form as those of the bear. The eyebrows thickly shade the small, quick–moving eyes. His stomach is the same as that of the brute. Upon his neck is a long mark that resembles a healed knife wound. When excited or angry it becomes flaming red. The muscles of the arm are placed upon the back in place of the front portion. The collar bone is perfectly straight and forms a socket at the shoulder similar to that in the brain. The hip and leg is the same. The hands have five fingers and a thumb double-jointed at the base. The nail is split and the fingers are webbed down to the second joint. The feet are exact facsimiles of those of the bear, and the track formed by the hands and feet are the same as those made by the bear. In fact he walks on all fours, has the perfect movements and bones of a bear, is an image of brain in action, yet in flesh and intelligence he is a human being.

Mott and Sproul soon found that their captive could talk a few words and sentences and seemed to understand what they said. He seemed impatient to return to his cave. As the smoke died away the three entered the Man Bear's home. Evidence of woman's work was all about it. In one corner lay a pile of dirty blankets. In another corner was a similar couch. As they pulled down the cover of the first they started back in horror. A skeleton lay exposed to view. The bones covered only with debris of flesh and skin, the head still adorned with long black hair, showed it to be that of a female. Under the bed a book was seen protruding. It was a Bible and upon the blank leaves was written by a woman's hand the Man Bear's

EARLY HISTORY

"Whosoever shall find my boy treat him kindly as you shall hope for mercy hereafter.

"In the year 1857, I, Elena Meigham, was married to Mathieus Emheim, a French Settler of the province of New Brunswick. He was devotedly fond of me, and I returned his love with all the pure fervor of my nature. For a year we were happy as lovers only can be. Then he became addicted to drink and, with the wine his jealousy was aroused. In order to overcome this we moved to the outskirts and he became a woodcutter. One day he captured a little cub bear and presented it to me. It was as playful as a kitten, and I became as fond of it as if it was a pet dog. Seeing that my affection had gone out to the little bruin he began to torment it, thinking to annoy me. A gentleman rode by in the spring; asked for a drink of water. I gave it to him, and thanking me, he bowed low, kissed my hand and rode off. Mathieus returned just then. He would listen to no explanation. Grasping my pet bruin he drew his knife across his throat and threw its bleeding and dying body into my lap. The shock in the delicate condition I was in proved a terrible one. Fear and sorrow both filled my heart and mind.

Under it I suffered. Oh, so much! Oh, how much! Time passed on. My baby boy was born. The anger of the father was exemplified in the form of his off-spring. Stricken by remorse he plunged into debauchery and I found refuge from his cruelty here in this cave, a home in the mountain side. David is the boy's name, and his birthplace was Iron Bound Cove, Queen's County, New Brunswick."

This is the whole history of the Man Bear. Under Mr. Sproul's tuition he has improved in intelligence wonderfully. He was placed on exhibition in order to satisfy the medical profession. In Bannell's Museum, Broadway, New York City, hundreds of thousands visited the Man Bear during his stay of nearly a year. At Bannell's Opera House, Brighton Beach, twenty thousand persons passed before him in a single day.

At the museum in Pittsburgh, and in the largest halls of the principal cities of the East, he has attracted profound attention, as the columns of notices in the public areas will testify.

If the history of David, the Man Bear, has the effect of teaching man to be kind to woman, it will have accomplished a result which will, perhaps, make it worth more than the reader has invested in its purchase.

OPINIONS OF THE PRESS

If a curiosity is to be judged by the notices which are accorded it by the critical supervision of the Press of the land, then, indeed, must the Man Bear stand in the very highest ranks of the many living wonders which from time to time have been presented to the public. True it is that the singular blending of the brute and human should command attention. Usually however, it is necessary to urge the editor of a newspaper to see and judge for himself as to the true character of any object. No class of men have so many duties to perform as the journalist, none are more conscientious in the performance of such duties. Nearly every person has something which, in their judgment, should receive attention at their hands, and all are averse to paying for such service when it is possible to avoid it. Under such circumstances the Man Bear has every reason to be proud of the creditable notices which have been published about him in every journal published in towns where he has exhibited. In no case has any fee been asked. It has all been gratuitous on the part of the publisher, and is simply their tribute to a marvel of nature, whose importance, in their opinion, was of such a nature as to require their spreading information of it to their readers.

As the press of the great metropolis is only impressible by reason of merit or news, and being wholly unapproachable by mercenary means, its expressions carry weight wherever they are read. Their opinions we give at length, knowing that they will be appreciated by all who may have seen the Man Bear, or who may have read or heard of his history.

THE NEW YORK SUN

"The history attached to one of the latest wonders introduced at Bunnell's Museum is full of pathetic interest. The growling and peculiar 'wish' of the bruin is painfully reproduced by the poor creature who rejoices in the name of the 'Boy Bear'. The story told by the lecturer evidently is given in good faith. The lecturer, Dr. Sproul, is one of the captors of the boy, who has been under his personal supervision. The brutality of the father to the mother, and the result as seen in the misshapen and half–intellectual offspring, should teach a lesson with a moral so strong that even the blind could read it."

THE NEW YORK HERALD

"Physicians and those interested in the study of the development of man should by all means visit the Broadway Museum. In one of the lower halls will be found a curious object denominated by those in charge as the Man Bear. It is claimed for him, that in intelligence and flesh he has all the attributes of human kind, but that in all movements and formation of the bones he resembles the bear. He certainly commanded attention from the fact that this strange admixture of the brute and human comes not from amalgamation in the inception of the monstrosity is simply to be attributed to the fright of the mother while in the first stages of pregnancy. It has often been questioned whether or not the mother's mind could be influenced to such an extent as to guide in formation of body or character of the mind the unborn child. In this case it is certain, if the story told by the descriptive lecturer be true, that the brutality of the jealous father in killing and throwing a bleeding cub into the lap of his wife has produced what is certainly a most curious and strange object."

THE NEW YORK STAR

The latest real curious and most mysterious object that eccentric Dame Nature has turned out has just been introduced at G.B. Bunnell's Museum. It is claimed to be half man and half bear. The history is plausible and related in most convincing manner by the captor of the Nondescript, Dr. Sproul. Davey, the Boy Bear, has really arrived at man's estate as he is now in his twenty-third year. He was born in Iron Bound Cove, New Brunswick. The name Boy Bear implies that he is the progeny of half brute, half man. Such is not the case, his father being of French descent, his mother of Irish parentage. Angered by jealousy the father cut the throat of a pet cub of the mother and then threw its dying, quivering carcass into the woman's lap. The result of his passion was the birth of the monster who is now attracting thousands of visitors to the museum each day. Davey is not an idiot by any means: he understands all that is said to him, and is fond of frightening with his savage growls and ugly display of teeth the over confident young men who think he is put upon the platform to play a part."